Forging Peace

Forging Peace

The Challenge of Central America

RICHARD R. FAGEN

Foreword by
George McGovern

A PACCA Book

Basil Blackwell

Copyright © PACCA 1987

First published 1987

Basil Blackwell Inc.
432 Park Avenue South, Suite 1503
New York, NY 10016, USA

Basil Blackwell Ltd
108 Cowley Road, Oxford, OX4 1JF, UK

British Library Cataloguing in Publication Data

Fagen, Richard R.
  Forging peace: the challenge of central
  America.—(A PACCA book).
  1. Central America—Foreign relations—
  United States   2. United States—Foreign
  relations—Central America
  I. Title
  327′.09728   F1436.8.U6
  ISBN 0-631-15854-5
  ISBN 0-631-15858-8 Pbk

Library of Congress Cataloging in Publication Data

Fagen, Richard R.
  Forging peace.
  "A PACCA book."
  Includes index.
  1. Central America—Politics and government—1979–
2. United States—Foreign relations—United States.
I. Title.
F1439.5.F34   1987   327.730728   87-17870
  ISBN 0-631-15854-5
  ISBN 0-631-15858-8 (pbk.)

Typeset in 11 on 13pt Plantin
by Joshua Associates Limited, Oxford
Printed in the USA

Contents

Contents

Part III An Alternative U.S. Policy

Foreword by George McGovern

During World War II, I flew a bomber in 35 missions against Nazi targets. I saw members of my crew and squadron die; once I had to feather three of my engines to get back to base. But for all of war's horrors, I would volunteer for combat again if another aggressor threatened the foundations of our civilization.

We as a people have never been afraid to fight for our own liberties, or to shed blood for the liberty of others. But in recent decades this willingness to fight for freedom has been abused, if not betrayed, by presidents who have portrayed wars to suppress indigenous revolutions as struggles against global tyranny.

On August 5, 1964, the Johnson administration provoked—or perhaps fabricated—a naval incident off the coast of North Vietnam. Two days later, along with 97 other senators, I voted for a resolution giving the administration permission to take "all necessary measures" to prosecute the Vietnam War. Knowing that the American public and Congress would never support their policy if it were explained openly, the Johnson and Nixon administrations continued to mislead the Congress and the public.

Today we are being misled about U.S. policy in Central America by the Reagan administration. Once again the United States is working to defeat peasant revolutionaries who represent not the slightest threat to our values or freedoms, and who indeed are fighting for many of the same things our forefathers fought for more than 200 years ago. The primary victims of the Reagan administration's decision to roll back revolution in

Central America are the Salvadoran villagers bombed and strafed by U.S.-made aircraft and the Nicaraguan civilians killed by U.S.-financed contra terrorists.

But the United States suffers too. When a president habitually misleads the American people and Congress and pursues a foreign policy contrary to this country's values, our constitutional system of checks and balances is subverted and our democratic principles are undermined. When a president who has never seen combat except on the screen draws us into an unpopular war, government is no longer responsive or even responsible. Just as it did in the 1960s, such irresponsibility at the highest levels threatens to tear apart the social fabric of this country.

Our country was born of a revolution against foreign tyranny and unrepresentative government. Today, revolution is still the only way for many Third World peoples to begin making their own history. It is time we got off their backs. And it is time that our government begin making policy that responds to "the better angels of our nature," as Abraham Lincoln said.

As the administration's Central America policy crumbles amid sordid revelations of arms smuggling, drug trafficking, and rampant illegality, we need a clear alternative that respects the law and our values. If the Congress, and our next president, are going to reject covert intervention, surrogate war, and systematic deceit, they will need new ideas like those contained in this book. PACCA's *Forging Peace* demonstrates that a policy based on respect rather than arrogance, diplomacy rather than war, and openness rather than secrecy, is practical as well as noble. PACCA's *Changing Course*, published in 1984, challenged the Kissinger Commission's contention that a military policy could act as a shield to bring democracy and development to the region. Now this book points the way to a realistic new policy.

Though I hope that this country is never faced with another Nazi aggressor, I know that we will not flinch from the challenge if our freedoms are again endangered. But let us have the wisdom to distinguish our friends from our enemies, and not to make war when we should make peace.

Preface and Acknowledgements

Forging Peace is a project of Policy Alternatives for the Caribbean and Central America (PACCA), an association of scholars and policymakers. Through research, analysis, policy recommendations, and the collaboration of experts in North America, Central America, and the Caribbean, PACCA aims to promote humane and democratic alternatives to present U.S. policies toward Central America and the Caribbean.

In 1984, PACCA produced *Changing Course: Blueprint for Peace in Central America and the Caribbean*, which presented a comprehensive alternative policy for peace and development. It has been endorsed by over 300 scholars in the field of Latin American studies, as well as over 100 prominent political, church, and labor leaders. *Changing Course* presented the basic platform for all PACCA's educational materials.

"U.S. foreign policy should be based on the principles which it seeks to further in the world. These include: non-intervention, respect for self-determination, collective self-defense, peaceful settlement of disputes, respect for human rights, support for democratic development and concern for democratic values. Adherence to these principles is critical to working out practical programs for regional peace and development."

The initial drafts of *Forging Peace* were prepared by a working group at Stanford University headed by Professor Terry Karl and myself. The other members of the working group were Bradford Barham, Kathleen Foote Durham, Raul Hinojosa, Shelley McConnell, and Janice Thomson. Xabier Gorostiaga,

Preface and Acknowledgements

from PACCA's counterpart in Central America and the Caribbean, CRIES (Coordinador Regional de Investigaciones Económicas y Sociales), made important contributions at both the initial and subsequent stages of the drafting process.

Additional materials were prepared by Robert Borosage, John Cavanagh, Saul Landau, William LeoGrande, and Colin Danby, PACCA's publications coordinator. Michael Czerny, from PACCA's sister organization, CAPA (Canada-Caribbean-Central America Policy Alternatives), provided a critical final editing of the text.

During the process of drafting and revision the following people contributed immeasurably with comments and suggestions: Robert Armstrong, Deborah Barry, Philip Berryman, Morris Blachman, Philippe Bourgois, Philip Brenner, Cindy Buhl, Judy Butler, Jefferson Boyer, Charles Carreras, Norma Chinchilla, Joshua Cohen, Betsy Cohn, Michael Conroy, Mark Cook, Carmen Diana Deere, Tim Draimin, Cameron Duncan, Diana Dunham, Marc Edelman, Ricardo Falla, Richard Feinberg, E. V. K. Fitzgerald, Heather Foote, Hank Frundt, Dennis Gilbert, Chris Gjording, Eva Gold, Nora Hamilton, Frank LaRue, Jennifer Logan, Bob Malone, Beatriz Manz, Peter Marchetti, Jim Morrell, Richard Newfarmer, Manuel Pastor, Juan Hernández Pico, David Reed, Debra Reuben, Joel Rogers, Mark Rosenberg, Jocelyn Rotter, Patricia Rotter, Patricia Rumer, Helen Safa, Joaquín Samayoa, Angela Sanbrano, Kenneth Sharpe, Philip Shepherd, Jan Shinpoch, Eric Shultz, Dan Siegel, Holly Sklar, Robert Styx, Marge Swedish, Julie Sweig, John Weeks, Patrick Wictor, and Michael Zalkin. In particular special thanks are owed to Robert Stark, PACCA's Executive Director, for his invaluable contributions.

Forging Peace has been made possible by grants and donations from the following foundations and organizations: The Arca Foundation, The Boehm Foundation, The William and Flora Hewlett Foundation, The Joint Foundation Support, Albert Kunstadter Family Foundation, The Andrew W. Mellon Foundation, The National Community Funds, The Norman

Foundation, The Ottinger Foundation, The Samuel Rubin Foundation, The William H. Vanderbilt Foundation, The Youth Project, The Center for Research in International Studies and the Center for Latin American Studies (both of Stanford University), The Committee on Latin America and the Caribbean of the National Council of Churches, and The Women's Division of Global Ministries of the United Methodist Church.

For the most of the period during which I was working on *Forging Peace*, I was partially supported by a fellowship from the John Simon Guggenheim Memorial Foundation. Needless to say, neither that Foundation, nor any of the other organizations mentioned, is in any way responsible for the content of this report or the opinions expressed herein.

The same cannot be said, however, for the dozens of individuals listed above, and the unnamed others who have given us advice, counsel, and encouragment. My name appears as author only because the cover was not large enough to include the names of all those who contributed. *Forging Peace* is truly a cooperative effort. In this it reflects in microcosm our hopes for the hemisphere and our beliefs about the future: If lasting peace is to come to Central America, all women and men of vision, courage, and goodwill, North Americans as well as Latin Americans, must contribute. There is work enough for everyone.

Richard Fagen,
Co-Chair, PACCA Executive Board

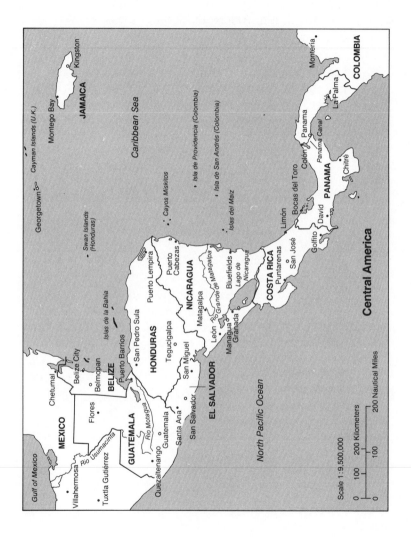

Gulf of Mexico

MEXICO

Villahermosa
Tuxtla Gutiérrez
Río Usumacinta

Chetumal

Belize City
Belmopan
BELIZE
Puerto Barrios

Flores

Islas de la Bahía

GUATEMALA
Quezaltenango
Río Motagua
Guatemala
Santa Ana
San Salvador
EL SALVADOR
San Miguel

San Pedro Sula
HONDURAS
Tegucigalpa

Puerto Lempira

Puerto
Cabezas

NICARAGUA
Matagalpa
León
Río Grande de Matagalpa
Managua
Granada
Lago de
Nicaragua
Bluefields

North Pacific Ocean

COSTA RICA
Puntarenas
San José
Golfito
Limón

Bocas del Toro
Colón
David
PANAMA
Panama
Panama Canal
Chitré
La Palma

Montería

COLOMBIA

Georgetown
Cayman Islands (U.K.)

Swan Islands
(Honduras)

Cayos Miskitos

Isla de Providencia (Colombia)

Isla de San Andrés (Colombia)

Islas del Maíz

Caribbean Sea

Montego Bay
JAMAICA
Kingston

Scale 1:9,500,000

0   100   200 Kilometers
0   100   200 Nautical Miles

Central America

PART I

Toward a Solution to the Central American Crisis

1

The Problem

Without peace there can be no development, and without development there can be no peace. We must break this vicious circle.

Belisario Betancur, president of Colombia, 1984[1]

United States policy toward Central America has been a disaster for the citizens of that war-torn region, and for the United States as well. If this policy is not changed, the situation will get worse, not better, both at home and abroad. We need to understand what has gone wrong, and what the United States must do—and stop doing. We need the courage and vision to make the required changes.

A false doctrine of U.S. national security dominates official thinking. In its extreme form, this doctrine sees any government in the region that is not shaped by and beholden to the United States as a threat to our vital interests. The fundamental assumption is that the region is so volatile and unstable, and the Soviet Union so aggressive and wily, that sooner or later our enemies will gain a foothold on the American land mass, threatening not only Panama to the south, but also Mexico and, eventually, the United States to the north.

Today Nicaragua, says the administration, tomorrow all of Central America, and then the Canal and Mexican oil. As President Reagan, in arguing for aid to the contras in the summer of 1986, ominously put it,

> Think again how Cuba became a Soviet air and naval base. You will see what Nicaragua will look like if we continue to do nothing. Cuba became a Soviet base gradually over many years. There was no single dramatic event. ... And so it will be with Nicaragua. Eventually ... we will have to confront the reality of a Soviet military beachhead inside our defense perimeters—about 500 miles from Mexico.[2]

This endlessly repeated refrain has proven useful to the Reagan administration in two ways. On the one hand, it justifies an increasingly aggressive U.S. policy of militarizing the region; on the other, it deflects public attention from the pressing economic and social problems of Central America. Further, since the alleged threat depends on actions yet to happen, it is extremely difficult to disprove.

Since the early 1980s, the chosen instrument of U.S. policy in Central America has been "low-intensity conflict,"[3] a strategy based on waging an integrated economic, political, cultural, and military struggle, using local resources to the greatest extent possible while avoiding the overt use of U.S. combat troops. What looks like low-intensity conflict from the United States, however, is what one Special Forces officer called "total war at the grass-roots level."[4]

To an administration attempting to minimize opposition at home among citizens still sensitive to the human and material costs of the Vietnam debacle, one of the most attractive features of this type of conflict is that it is not immediately perceived as costly or devastating in the United States. But the conflict that Central Americans are experiencing today is far from "low-intensity." Since 1980, perhaps 140,000 people, or one out of every 200 residents of the region, have died in war-related violence.[5] Casualties of the same proportion in the United States would leave over 1 million dead.

The strategy has been immensely costly in other ways as well. National security pursued through the militarization of the region has deepened the already-existing development crisis in

Central America, led to more rather than less foreign involvement, and brought hardship, dislocation, and death to hundreds of thousands of Central Americans. It has also produced 3 million Central American refugees,[6] a prolonged civil war in El Salvador, a brutal but ineffectual contra army fighting against the Sandinista government in Nicaragua, physical damage and lost production running to billions of dollars;[7] and still there is no end in sight to regional tensions, poverty, or violence. Allies have been alienated, billions of U.S. tax dollars wasted, and immense amounts of human and material resources diverted from other problems at home, in Latin America, and elsewhere.

Is there a better way? Can an alternative U.S. policy contribute to development and peace in Central America while simultaneously satisfying fundamental U.S. and regional security concerns? The answer is yes—but *priorities must be reversed*. Events have shown that the militarization of the region will bring neither security nor development. To continue down the path already taken will cost billions more—and if current conflicts lead to full-scale U.S. armed intervention, perhaps thousands of American lives as well. How can this additional disaster be avoided?

The answer can be simply stated: A policy of demilitarization and negotiations must replace the current policy of war. This fundamental guideline does not tell the entire story, however. Demilitarization and negotiations, unless accompanied by a vigorous program of regional development and increased social justice and democracy, will not lead to a sustainable peace.

This additional point is vitally important. Observers of many political persuasions agree that the vast economic inequalities of the region are at the root of the current upheaval.[8] The area's dominant economic model, based on agricultural exports and controlled by a small elite, produced significant economic growth from the 1950s through the 1970s. But this growth brought further impoverishment, not increased well-being, to the majority of the region's citizens. And when world recession

5

and spiraling debt hit Central America in the 1970s and 1980s, the poor were further squeezed. In response, broadly based popular organizations began seeking more equitable distribution of the fruits of growth and struggling to end dictatorial regimes.

These movements, fueled by nationalism and supported by a popular Christianity that defends the rights of the poor, represent a fundamental political shift in a region long ruled (with the partial exception of Costa Rica) by entrenched elites. Today, the old political and economic formulas have been discredited; a new model, combining social justice and democracy with economic growth, must be found.

The task will not be easy, nor will the price be cheap, but by now one thing has become absolutely clear: *A new model of development cannot be constructed under conditions of war*. Peace is a prerequisite for development, and without development there can be no long-term stability.

Thus the circle closes: Without negotiations and demilitarization, there can be no reconstruction of the economies and societies of the region; without reconstruction, there can be neither economic growth nor enhanced political participation and social justice; without growth, participation, and justice, there can be no lasting peace and no political stability. And as realistic Americans will recognize, true security, both north and south, depends ultimately on the construction of prosperous, just, and vigorous economic and political systems throughout the hemisphere. In the absence of such changes, no amount of troops or hardware can prevent the tragedies of the 1980s from being replayed with ever more violence, destruction, and foreign involvement in the 1990s and beyond.

Notes

[1] Quoted in Richard E. Feinberg and Bruce M. Bagley, *Development Postponed: The Political Economy of Central America in the 1980s* (Boulder, Colo.: Westview, 1986), 47.

The Problem

2 *The New York Times*, 25 June 1986.

3 For a discussion of low-intensity conflict in the 1980s, see Sara Miles, "The Real War: Low Intensity Conflict in Central America," in NACLA, *Report on the Americas* 20 (April/May, 1986): 17–48; and Tom Barry, *Low Intensity Conflict: The New Battlefield in Central America* (Albuquerque: The Resource Center, 1986). See also, William M. LeoGrande, "Central America: Counterinsurgency Revisited," in NACLA, *Report on the Americas* 21 (January–February): 3–5.

4 Miles, NACLA, op. cit.: 19.

5 An estimated 110,000–140,000 Central Americans have died since 1980. This figure includes 60,000 in El Salvador since 1980, 36,000–72,000 in Guatemala between 1981 and 1984, and 12,000 in Nicaragua between 1980 and 1985. For El Salvador, see *Washington Post*, 4 June 1986. For Guatemala, see George Black, "Under the Gun," in NACLA, *Report on the Americas* 19 (November/December 1985): 11; and *Central America Report* 12 (22 February 1985): 52. Also see Chris Krueger and Kjell Enge's *Security and Development Conditions in the Guatemalan Highlands* (Washington, D.C.: Washington Office on Latin America, August 1985), which estimates 50,000–70,000 killed between 1978 and 1985. For Nicaragua, see *Central America Report* 12 (6 December 1985): 370; and *Mesoamerica* 4 (October 1985): 3.

6 Of this 3 million, 1.2 million were Salvadoran, 1.1 million were Guatemalan, and 0.3 million were Nicaraguan. For El Salvador, see Patricia Ruggles and Michael Fix, *Impacts and Potential Impacts of Central American Migrants on HHS and Related Programs of Assistance* (Washington, D.C.: Urban Institute, September 1985), 9, 46; AID internal memo, "El Salvador Displaced Persons Program," 15 November 1985; and Washington Office on Latin America, "Common Questions on El Salvador: The War and Human Rights," Winter 1986: 5. For Guatemala, see Americas Watch Committee, *Guatemala: News In Brief* 1 (February–April 1986): 5; Guatemalan Church in Exile, *Development: The New Face of War* 6 (April 1986): 21; and Guatemala Human Rights Commission, *General Report on the Human Rights Situation in Guatemala, January–May 1986, 8th General Assembly CODEHUCA*, 8–9. For Nicaragua, see Ruggles and Fix, op. cit., 9, 10, 46.

7 For El Salvador, see *Washington Post*, 12 December 1983; and *Central America Report* 12 (26 July 1985): 237–38. For Nicaragua, see E. V. K. Fitzgerald, "An Evaluation of the Economic Costs to Nicaragua of U.S. Aggression: 1980–1984," in Rose J. Spalding, ed., *The Political Economy of Revolutionary Nicaragua* (Boston: Allen & Unwin, 1987); and *Central America Report* 12 (6 December 1985): 370.

8 See, for example, *Report of the President's National Bipartisan Commission on Central America*, foreword by Henry A. Kissinger (New York: Macmillan, 1984), Chapter 3.

7

2
The Record

I ask that, if you truly want to defend human rights, you:
—Prohibit military aid to the Salvadoran government;
—Guarantee that your government will not intervene,
directly or indirectly, with military, economic or diplomatic
pressure in determining the destiny of the Salvadoran people.

Archbishop Oscar A. Romero, in a letter to President
Jimmy Carter, February 1980—one month before
Romero's assassination while saying mass[1]

When we look at Central America today, a region with approximately one-tenth the total population of the United States and less than 1 percent of the U.S. gross national product, what do we see?

We see, most tragically, a region devastated by war. As pointed out in Chapter 1, up to 140 thousand Central Americans have died in war-related incidents since 1980 and 3 million Central Americans, or 15 percent of the region's total population, have become refugees. War continues to wrack Nicaragua and El Salvador. With the contras clearly unable to defeat the Sandinistas, and the Salvadoran army unable to defeat the FMLN insurgents, peace is nowhere in sight. Regional tensions are at a flashpoint, local armies and guerrilla forces continue to grow, and foreign military involvement is at an all-time high.[2]

Further, not only has economic development come to a halt, but most countries have suffered economic *deterioration*. For the region as a whole, per capita income dropped by almost one-third between 1978 and 1985.[3] During the first half of the 1980s, the regional decline in real wages, combined with extensive unemployment and inflation, meant that living standards fell by as much as 50 percent for the majority of Central Americans. The welfare implications of such a huge reduction in living standards are even more staggering when viewed in light of the fact that in 1980 almost two-thirds of all Central Americans were already classified as living in poverty, and over 40 percent as living in extreme poverty.[4] Moreover, by the mid-1980s the region's foreign debt totaled almost $15 billion, or over $600 per person.[5]

War has dramatically exacerbated economic deterioration. An estimated $3 billion in private capital had fled Central America by 1982, and much more has followed since then.[6] The wars in El Salvador and Nicaragua have destroyed property and disrupted production to the tune of an additional $2–3 billion.[7] Although some capital flight, debt, unemployment, and economic dislocation would have occurred during the recessionary years of the 1980s in any event, war-induced political tensions and military conflicts have significantly deepened the crisis.

Finally, democracy, one of Washington's most frequently proclaimed goals, remains a distant dream. Although generals have been replaced by elected civilian presidents in Honduras, El Salvador, and Guatemala, in all three cases the nominal governments exercise only marginal power.

The U.S. Illusion

Supporters of current policy argue that the Reagan administration has been successful in Central America because the Salvadoran and Guatemalan insurgents have not come to power and the Nicaraguan revolution has been put on the defensive. But these claims are based on a narrow, misleading, and ultimately very dangerous definition of national security.

Toward a Solution to the Crisis

Throughout most of U.S. history, national security has traditionally and legitimately been defined as the protection of the territorial integrity and fundamental values of the United States. But after World War II, security became identified with virulent anticommunism and, by extension, with the containment and elimination of any significant movement for radical change overseas. In a tragic perversion of our own history, the most innovative 18th-century experiment in self-governance became the global opponent of national liberation and self-governance in today's newly emerging countries.

In a troubled and very unequal world, however, long-term security depends not on "holding the line," but on economic development, social justice, and political systems able to accommodate needed changes. In the complex and risky system of superpower rivalry, moreover, security depends on the support of allies, the capacity to exert influence by nonmilitary means, and the exercise of statecraft to reduce tensions and foreign military involvement in areas of existing conflict. Perhaps most importantly, security also requires policies that are widely supported at home. When security is assessed in this broader and more realistic fashion, the administration's record looks very different indeed.

After his inauguration, President Reagan sharply escalated the military component of U.S. foreign policy in Central America. In 1981, Washington launched a campaign of threats against Cuba, initiated a covert war against Nicaragua, and substantially increased military aid to El Salvador. In 1982, U.S. aid to the Salvadoran military doubled; in 1983 the United States constructed four military bases in Honduras and began maneuvers that brought thousands of U.S. troops to Central America. In 1984, military aid to El Salvador doubled again (and this time included AC-47 gunships), and the CIA mined the harbors of Nicaragua. In 1985, Green Beret advisers were sent to lightly armed—and formally neutral—Costa Rica. In 1986, military aid grants to Guatemala were resumed.[8]

This policy of militarization did not go unnoticed. Both Cuba and the Soviet Union responded to U.S. threats and actions against Nicaragua by increasing their military aid to that country. By 1984 the U.S.S.R. had supplied hundreds of thousands of rifles and millions of rounds of ammunition, along with tanks and helicopter gunships, to the Sandinistas. The U.S.-financed contra war against Nicaragua and the administration's increasingly open threats to use U.S. armed might in force have pushed Nicaragua into a closer military and economic relationship with the very powers that Washington claimed it was trying to keep out of the region.[9]

America's European and Canadian allies have overwhelmingly opposed the U.S.-sponsored contra war, condemned U.S. violations of international law, and refused to participate in the U.S. economic embargo against Nicaragua. In fact, while the U.S. share of Nicaragua's trade was dropping from 30 percent in 1980 to 7 percent in 1985, Western European, Japanese, and Canadian trade with Nicaragua was increasing.[10] Preferential economic assistance continues to flow from Europe to Nicaragua, and many European nations have warned the United States that direct intervention in the region would be a disaster.[11]

The heart of the European and Canadian critique is that U.S. actions are both wrong and counterproductive. Former Spanish foreign minister Fernando Morán best expressed the collective view of our allies when he said, "We belong to the West because we feel that the values which underlie the way of life and the political systems of the West are superior to all others; and we believe that by mining ports, financing armies of contras, and supporting regimes which allow death squads, one is not defending the West, but rather undermining its foundations."[12]

Latin American disagreements with U.S. policy are even more fundamental. Mexico, Venezuela, Colombia, and Panama, the original Contadora countries,* were joined by the powerful support group of Argentina, Brazil, Uruguay, and Peru in

---

* A group that called for a negotiated settlement of Central American conflicts following a meeting on Contadora Island, off Panama, in 1983. See Chapter 5 for details.

denouncing the 1986 decision to send $100 million to the contras. As democratically governed nations in the hemisphere, they have sound reason to fear the violation of international law and standards involved in U.S. support for a terrorist army dedicated to overthrowing a legitimate government. These countries' support for a negotiated settlement and for demilitarization—as embodied in the Contadora proposals—has been unwavering.

But regional tensions, generated by a narrowly military foreign policy in Central America, have other implications as well. Latin America has not yet emerged from the economic depression that hastened the collapse of military dictatorships in the early 1980s. The stability of the new civilian governments of South America—and of Mexico as well—is threatened by the imposition of harsh austerity measures on a population whose standard of living has already suffered a serious decline. Up to 50 percent of some countries' export earnings goes to pay the interest on foreign debt;[13] almost nothing remains for development or programs of social welfare.

Nevertheless, Washington's fixation on Central America has meant that more than half of U.S. aid for all Latin America in the 1980s has gone to only three small countries—Costa Rica, Honduras, and El Salvador—which have less than 4 percent of Latin America's total population.[14] This aid policy has been widely perceived among U.S. allies in the hemisphere as an inexcusable distortion of proper priorities. While urgent developmental needs in the still-fragile democracies of South America have gone unmet, hundreds of millions of dollars have been poured into military programs in Central America.

Meanwhile, Central America's real problems not only remain unsolved, but continue to worsen. As summarized in the 1986 report of the Inter-American Dialogue, "These bloody struggles [in Central America] not only hinder democratic development in the nations immediately involved; they also fuel the polarization and the militarization of neighboring countries. If the conflict in Central America continues to escalate, its effects may well spill over to poison the politics of South America as well."[15] This prospect hardly enhances the security of either the United States or its neighbors in the hemisphere.

The Costs at Home

Washington's policy toward Central America also has taken a large toll at home. Not surprisingly, the real dollar costs have been minimized and understated by an administration anxious to have Americans believe that not much money is being spent in or on the region. Although U.S. assistance to Costa Rica, Honduras, El Salvador, and Guatemala in 1985 was officially reported as approximately $1.3 billion,[16] the total dollar costs actually were much higher. One source estimated that "the costs of all the naval and ground exercises, of the military construction, and of the forces based in the region . . . would run to more than $3 billion a year."[17] When the $1.3 billion in direct assistance for 1985 is added to this figure, the total is more than three times the administration's estimate. If this $4.3 billion were divided up among the 21 million citizens of Central America, everyone's income would rise by more than $200.

Fundamental damage is also being done to basic American values. To pursue policies that are rejected by majorities in every poll of U.S. public opinion, the administration has woven a tissue of lies and half-truths and flouted national and international law. The White House originally secured congressional funding for the contras under the pretense that the purpose of the contra army was to interdict arms being sent to the Salvadoran guerrillas, despite the open declarations of contra leaders that their intent was to overthrow the Sandinistas.[18] Shortly thereafter, in December 1982, Congress passed the Boland amendment, prohibiting the use of U.S. funds "for the purpose of overthrowing the government of Nicaragua."

For two-and-a-half years, until the amendment lapsed, the administration continued to finance the contra army, sometimes clandestinely, claiming that its purpose was only to "apply pressure" to the Sandinistas. When the CIA mined Nicaragua's ports in the fall of 1984, the contras received instructions to claim responsibility. Bases intended for use against Nicaragua were constructed in Honduras under the fiction that they were only temporary facilities needed for U.S. maneuvers.[19]

The scandal that broke in November 1986 over the illegal diversion of arms sales profits to the contras was the logical consequence of a foreign policy characterized by deception and lawbreaking. Whatever President Reagan and other high officials knew about the details of contra funding, it is clear that in their determination to pursue a military solution in Central America, they broke U.S. and international law, ignored treaty commitments and the U.S. Constitution, and manipulated and lied to the Congress and the public.

In the conflict between power and principles in international politics, the United States has historically claimed to occupy a special place. As a nation founded on the proposition that laws, not individuals, should rule, it has presented itself as a principled Great Power, respectful of treaties, neighbors, and international obligations and constantly seeking ways to support rather than subvert a rule-respecting international order. If the reality has not always lived up to the promise, the self-perception has nevertheless been widespread that we are better than those we criticize.

Unfortunately, U.S. relations with Central America, and particularly with Nicaragua, tell a very different story. The 1986 judgment of the World Court thoroughly documents the U.S. government's multiple attempts to damage and overthrow a neighboring government. In the process, Washington violated not only the Geneva Convention and the charters of the United Nations and the Organization of American States, but also the most fundamental principles of the peaceful settlement of disputes.[20] Nor is the Congress blameless. In approving aid to the contras, Congress has cooperated with the administration in its search for military solutions to Central American problems.

The record speaks for itself: After years of intense U.S.

involvement in the region and the spending of billions of dollars, neither Central America's future prospects nor U.S. or regional security have been advanced. Official Washington is lying to the American people, and U.S. policies violate the principles and treaties that we were once instrumental in promoting.

Notes

[1] Marvin E. Gettleman, et al., eds., *El Salvador: Central America in the New Cold War*, rev. ed. (New York: Grove, 1987), 134.

[2] In addition, elements of the Israeli, Taiwanese, and—until recently—Argentine security forces have operated in the region. Some have suggested that Libya and the PLO have also been involved. See David F. Ronfeldt, "Rethinking the Monroe Doctrine," *Orbis* 28 (Winter 1985): 689.

[3] Richard E. Feinberg and Bruce M. Bagley, *Development Postponed: The Political Economy of Central America in the 1980s* (Boulder, Colo.: Westview, 1986), 5.

[4] United Nations Economic Commission for Latin America, *Central America: Nature of the Present Economic Crisis, the Challenges It Raises and the International Cooperation for Which It Calls*, E/CEPAL/CCE/402/Rev. 1 (26 August 1981), 2.

[5] *World Development Report 1986* (New York: World Bank, 1986), 208–209.

[6] Richard E. Feinberg and Robert A. Pastor, "Far From Hopeless: An Economic Program for Post-War Central America," in Robert S. Leiken, ed., *Central America: Anatomy of Conflict* (New York: Pergamon Press, 1984), 201. Also see Xabier Gorostiaga, "Towards Alternative Policies for the Region," in George Irvin and Xabier Gorostiaga, eds., *Towards an Alternative for Central America and the Caribbean* (Boston: George Allen & Unwin, 1985), 14. Accurate figures on capital flight since 1982 are not available.

[7] See Chapter 1, footnote 7.

[8] For a good, brief description of the evolution of the Reagan administration's Central America policies through 1983, see Christopher Dickey, "Central America: From Quagmire to Cauldron?" *Foreign Affairs* 62 (January 1984): 659–94.

[9] A U.S. Intelligence Report prepared in late 1984 concluded that "the overall [Nicaraguan] buildup is primarily defense oriented, and much of the recent effort has been devoted to improving counter insurgency capabilities." See the *Wall Street Journal*, 3 April 1985. For a discussion of the role of the Soviets and Cubans in the region, see Edmé Domínguez Reyes, "Soviet Relations With Central America, the Caribbean, and Members of the Contadora Group," *Annals of the American Academy* 481 (September 1985): 147–58. See also C. G. Jacobsen, *Soviet Attitudes Towards Aid to and Contacts With Central American Revolutionaries*, a report for the Department of State, June 1984.

[10] Center for International Policy and the Overseas Development Council, "The U.S. Embargo Against Nicaragua—One Year Later," *Policy Focus* 1986 (3): 3.

[11] Daniel Siegel and Tom Spaulding with Peter Kornbluh, *Outcast Among Allies: The International Costs of Reagan's War Against Nicaragua* (Washington, D.C.: Institute for Policy Studies, November 1985), 11–16. See also Joseph Cirincione, ed., *Central America and the Western Alliance* (New York: Holmes & Meier, 1985).

[12] Siegel and Spaulding, op. cit., 18. See also Canadian Prime Minister Brian Mulroney's address to the Inter-American Press Association, Vancouver, British Columbia, 15 September 1986.

[13] Abraham F. Lowenthal, "Threat and Opportunity in the Americas," *Foreign Affairs* 64 (1986): 546; and Pedro-Pablo Kuczynski, "Latin American Debt: Act Two," *Foreign Affairs* 62 (Fall 1983): 20.

[14] House of Representatives Committee on Appropriations, *Foreign Assistance and Related Programs Appropriations for 1987*, Part I: 731, 740, 749, 758, 767, 785.

[15] *1986 Report of the Inter-American Dialogue* (Washington, D.C.: Aspen Institute of Humanistic Studies, April 1986), 31.

[16] Stephen R. Harper and Larry Q. Nowels, "Central America and U.S. Foreign Assistance: Issues for Congress," U.S. Library of Congress, Congressional Research Service, 24 July 1985, Issue Brief 84075, Appendix.

[17] Joshua Cohen and Joel Rogers, *Inequity and Intervention: The Federal Budget and Central America* (Boston: South End Press, 1986), 45.

[18] See Joanne Omang, "Rebel Fund Diversion Rooted in Early Policy," *Washington Post*, 1 January 1987. On U.S. public opinion, see William M. LeoGrande, *Central America and the Polls* (Washington, D.C.: Washington Office on Latin America, March 1987).

[19] On the Boland amendment and other questions of illegality, see *U.S. Policy in Central America: Against the Law? An Analysis of Possible Violations of 30 United States and International Laws* (Washington, D.C.: Arms Control and Foreign Policy Caucus, 11 September 1984).

[20] *Nicaragua v The United States of America*. Judgment of the International Court of Justice (The Hague, Netherlands: 27 June 1986).

3
Roots of the Crisis

The fundamental causes of dissatisfaction [in Central America] are the existing social, political, and economic inequities.

General Wallace Nutting,
retiring U.S. Army Chief of
the Southern Command, 1983[1]

The roots of the contemporary Central American crisis go far back in time—much further than most citizens and policy-makers in the United States are willing to look. The events of recent years, however, can be very deceiving. For almost three decades, from 1950 to 1978, Central America had one of the highest growth rates in the world. Gross domestic product was expanding at an average annual rate of at least 5 percent in all five countries (Costa Rica, Nicaragua, Honduras, El Salvador, Guatemala).[2] Fueling this rapid economic growth for most of that period were an expanding world economy, substantial foreign aid and investment, and regional policies of agricultural diversification, trade expansion, and local industrialization. Per capita income almost doubled during this period, new roads, dams, and schools were built, and literacy increased. Yet, by the end of the 1970s, Central America was in the grips of a profound economic and political crisis. What went wrong?

Old Crops, New Problems

Central Americans have always lived from the land. From the first incursions of the Spaniards in the 16th century, however, indigenous subsistence agriculture began to be squeezed out by export crops such as indigo. Communal and individual peasant farmers were gradually—often violently—displaced by a relatively small number of landowning families who controlled large estates. In the 20th century, this tiny agricultural elite, along with, in some cases, foreign corporate owners, dominated economic life by producing commodities—particularly coffee and bananas—for foreign markets. This pattern of huge plantations and crops for export is known as the agro-export model of development.

A primary feature of an agro-export economy is its dependence on a very few crops. In the 1920s, for example, coffee and bananas accounted for more than 70 percent of the export earnings in all five republics—and more than 90 percent in Costa Rica, El Salvador, and Guatemala. Even today, despite the addition of sugar, cotton, and cattle during the export diversification drive begun in the 1960s, the same two products account for more than half of all exports in every country except Nicaragua. In 1980, these five agricultural commodities accounted for more than 70 percent of Central America's total exports, and for more than one-third of the region's total gross domestic product.

Economies so dependent on a limited number of agricultural exports are extremely vulnerable to fluctuations in international demand and prices. A 25 percent drop in the world price of coffee will cost Central America $330 million in a typical year, representing an 8 percent loss in total export earnings. But because Central America accounts for only 13 percent of world coffee exports, the region exerts no major influence on world markets. Conversely, when the prices of imports rise relative to the prices of exports—as they frequently do in the case of agricultural commodities such as coffee and sugar—the region's economies also suffer greatly. The structural vulnerability of the agro-export model means that economic crises in the region are frequent and, over the long run, inevitable.

From the outset, the Central American version of the agro-export model generated an extremely unequal distribution of income and wealth. The process of wresting land from the local inhabitants and suppressing the subsequent revolts was violent, and the plantation owners financed armies and bought governments to keep the poor majority under control. By the 1930s, Nicaragua, El Salvador, Honduras, and Guatemala had succumbed to military rule characterized by the wholesale abuse of human rights and a total lack of political freedom.

In the contemporary era, this concentration of land and wealth has generated a self-reinforcing dynamic of inequality and neglect of industry. The majority of Central Americans, comprising peasants and landless workers with incomes insufficient to meet even their most basic needs, have not participated in the economy as consumers of manufactured products. Thus, industrial development to meet domestic demand has been minimal. At the other end of the social structure, the economic elites have had sufficient income to afford a lifestyle equal to that of the most privileged in developed countries, complete with costly imports from abroad to sustain a luxurious way of life.

In the 1950s the historic mix of exports began to change. Realizing that their future was not guaranteed by coffee and bananas, many within the economic elite began to expand cash crop production into sugar, cotton, and beef—all commodities best produced on extensive holdings. In the process, tens of thousands of small farmers were pushed off the land, further reducing the production of food crops.[3] By the 1970s a region that had once been virtually self-sufficient in basic foods was importing large quantities of corn, beans, and other grains. Not only did these imports put new pressures on foreign exchange reserves, but many Central Americans who once grew their own food now found that they were unable to earn enough to pay for the higher-priced imported foodstuffs.

By the end of the 1950s, some planners from the region, along with specialists working with the U.N. Economic Commission on Latin America, realized that the agro-export model of growth needed to be transformed, or at least modified. Their hope was that with the help of protective tariffs and the expansion of smaller national markets to a regional level, industrial and manufactured products that were now being imported could shortly be produced at home. Import substitution, it was hoped, would reduce the dominance of the agro-export component of the economy, and a new, more balanced and equitable model would emerge.

A central feature of the changed economic model was to be the Central American Common Market (CACM). And the CACM did encourage economic growth. Between 1960 and 1969, trade among Central American countries increased from 4 percent to 35 percent of the region's total trade. But the profit from the new system went primarily to the same groups that had profited under the old system. National elites, including much of the traditional agrarian elite, became junior economic partners of foreign corporations and banks and used regional trade expansion and import substitution policies chiefly as a means of securing strategic access to tariff-protected markets. Furthermore, the highly protected new industries turned out to be dependent on imports of both raw materials and machinery, and in general the products produced were not competitive outside the region. Thus, rather than improving the foreign exchange situation by generating new exports and cutting imports, the new industries often did just the reverse. In practice, then, the CACM failed to produce balanced and equitable development.

By the 1970s, successive oil shocks and the currency demands generated by imports of food, industrial inputs, and luxury goods placed foreign exchange reserves under significant pressure throughout the region. Export earnings from the agrarian sector simply could not keep up with the demand for dollars. Government efforts in several countries to increase the level of taxation were successfully resisted by elites. At a time when international banks were eager to lend, increased foreign borrowing seemed to offer a solution to the foreign exchange problem and a way to fund continuing growth. But this solution soon turned into yet another problem, as debt service joined the list of burdens that the local economies had to shoulder.

Thus, although growth continued well into the 1970s, the model had exhausted itself. Crises multiplied. Honduras withdrew from the CACM as a result of its five-day war with El Salvador in 1969, and the market was further weakened by the inability of debtor countries—particularly Honduras and Nicaragua—to pay their bills. As the economic and political situations became increasingly uncertain and unstable in the late 1970s, creditors and investors hesitated to increase their levels of exposure, and local capital fled to Europe and the United States. Growth slowed dramatically, unemployment soared, and millions of Central Americans found their already meager incomes even less adequate than they had been just a few years earlier.

Injustice and the Exhaustion of Nonviolence

If the growth generated through the late 1970s had been more equally distributed, the exhaustion of the agro-export model might not have resulted in such profound crises. But rather than improving during this period, the distribution of income deteriorated. In almost every case the poorer groups in Central America—who were already living in poverty in 1960—were relatively worse off in 1980. What had been a substantial success from the point of view of overall economic growth was a disaster for most citizens of the region.

By 1980 the richest 20 percent of the population was receiving between one-half and two-thirds of total national income, depending on the country. At the other end of the spectrum, the poor were receiving almost nothing at all. In El Salvador, for example, the poorest 20 percent of the population received only 2 percent of national income, or the equivalent of $46 a year in constant 1970 dollars. In contrast, the 20 percent at the top of the pyramid received, on average, 33 times that amount—two-thirds of all national income.[4]

Not surprisingly, efforts to broaden economic and political participation during this period were commonplace. New social forces not content with the status quo called for a wide variety of reforms. In rural areas, as the imposition of the agro-export model displaced tens of thousands of peasants from the land, new groups of politically conscious agricultural wage laborers were organized. Thousands of landless and jobless peasants migrated to the cities, swelling the shanty towns of the urban poor. New urban industries spawned an urban labor movement. Rapid population growth, the spread of schooling and the mass media, and the demonstration effect of both local and foreign wealth produced a younger, better-educated, and ultimately more frustrated population. Growth without equity, rising expectations, elite intransigence, and militarized repression had swollen the ranks of those who were calling for fundamental and far-reaching change in Central America. Universities, the Church, trade unions, and other grass-roots groups provided national leadership for these new social forces. Mass organizations, church-based communities, and political parties ranging from Christian Democrats to Social Democrats and Socialists were founded.

Except in Costa Rica, these new organizations and parties met with fierce and swift repression from existing elites and their military allies. The results of the 1972 Salvadoran presidential elections, in which José Napoleón Duarte's coalition was the clear winner, were canceled by the military, and Duarte was beaten and exiled. Petitions and demonstrations supporting reform were met with clubs and gas in some cases, bullets and bayonets in others. The Somoza family tightened its grip on

Nicaragua. In Guatemala the military killed thousands in recurrent waves of urban and rural slaughter.

As political polarization increased, large numbers of Central Americans came to view nonviolent reform as impossible, and new impetus was given to armed opposition groups. Such movements were not new, but the extent of their support certainly was. Although not all voices advocated violence, many people had come to believe that the old order would not yield peacefully, and that more than tinkering would be needed to correct the structural problems that had come to characterize the economies and societies of the region.

Notes

[1] *Wall Street Journal*, 20 July 1983.

[2] United Nations Economic Commission for Latin America, *Statistical Yearbook for Latin America*, selected years.

[3] Robert Williams, *Export Agriculture and the Crisis in Central America* (Chapel Hill, N.C.: University of North Carolina Press, 1986).

[4] See United Nations Economic Commission for Latin America, *The Crisis in Central America: Its Origins, Scope, and Consequences*, 15 September 1983.

4

U.S. Responses: Then and Now

The evidence has mounted that the Administration has no earthly idea how to address the region's many complex problems other than to escalate U.S. military involvement.
U.S. Senate minority leader Robert Byrd, 1986[1]

By the late 1970s the Nicaraguan revolution, increasing instability in other countries in the region, and mounting economic problems forced Central America to the attention of U.S. policymakers. Under the Reagan administration, Washington's response to this immensely complex and longstanding set of problems has been quite simple: While paying lip service to the underlying economic and political crisis in the region, the fundamental policy response has been, as Senator Byrd commented, to escalate U.S. military involvement.

How can one explain this destructively simple response to what is clearly an immensely complex crisis? Why does the U.S. government respond to misery and inequity with guns rather than development? In the most immediate sense, the answers must be sought in the beliefs, goals, and tactics of the Reagan administration. But as with the Central American crisis itself, the answers must also be sought in the tangled history of United States relations with Latin America in general, and with Central America in particular.

"We Do Control the Destinies . . ."

In 1927, Under Secretary of State Robert Olds spoke for many, then and now, when he said, "The Central American area down to and including the Isthmus of Panama constitutes a legitimate sphere of influence for the United States. . . . We do control the destinies of Central America, and we do so for the simple reason that the national interest absolutely dictates such a course."[2] In making this declaration, Olds not only summed up decades of history, but also articulated a presumption of hegemony that continues to this day. Beginning in the middle of the 19th century, as part of the ideology of the Monroe Doctrine and Manifest Destiny, U.S. filibusterers and entrepreneurs pushed relentlessly and often violently into the region in search of power and profits. In most instances, the U.S. government was not far behind.

In the present century the United States has projected its power and used military, diplomatic, and economic instruments to shape events in the region in a decidedly more systematic manner. The landing of the Marines in Nicaragua in 1909, the Woodrow Wilson administration's pressures on Costa Rica in support of U.S. oil interests, and the imposition of U.S. fiscal agents on El Salvador in 1921 were predictably justified as the inevitable right and duty of a Great Power to intervene in the internal affairs of its smaller neighbors.

With the advent of the Cold War, in the late 1940s, this long-standing U.S. presumption of right to rule in the hemisphere, and particularly in Central America, was given new energy and meaning by global policies of anticommunism and Soviet containment. For example, in 1950, at a meeting with U.S. ambassadors to Latin America, George Kennan (then working in the State Department) warned against the communist threat in language that is strikingly contemporary:

> The final answer might be an unpleasant one, but . . . we should not hesitate before police repression by the local government.

25

> This is not shameful since the Communists are essentially traitors. . . . It is better to have a strong regime in power than a liberal government if it is indulgent and relaxed and penetrated by Communists.[3]

The step from Kennan's position to the CIA-engineered overthrow of the reformist Jacobo Arbenz government in Guatemala in 1954 was easy enough, particularly in the context of more than a half-century of U.S. intervention in the region; so, too, was continued support for the Somoza dynasty in Nicaragua and the military regimes in El Salvador, Guatemala, and—most of the time—Honduras.

Anticommunism as the central doctrine of U.S. policy in Latin America and the Caribbean was given added impetus by the Cuban Revolution in 1959 and the failed attempt to overthrow Fidel Castro at the Bay of Pigs in 1961. Since the Missile Crisis of October 1962, the overriding goal of the Latin American policy of all U.S. administrations has been to avoid "another Cuba." The invasion of the Dominican Republic in 1965, the support of counterinsurgency warfare in Guatemala and elsewhere in the 1960s and 1970s, the destabilization of the Salvador Allende regime in Chile from 1970 to 1973, the response to the Nicaraguan insurrection of 1978–79, subsequent U.S. involvement in El Salvador, and the invasion of Grenada in 1983 all reflected this overriding priority—under Democratic as well as Republican administrations.

The Reagan administration, however, has given its own twist to these long-standing trends. First, whereas anticommunism and the containment of radical movements in the hemisphere have traditionally been pursued through a variety of policies, the central instrument of U.S. policy since 1980 has been military force unleashed in a complex strategy that marries local armies to U.S. money, technology, and tactics. The strong development thrust of President John F. Kennedy's Alliance for Progress, the diplomatic openings of the Richard Nixon and Gerald Ford administrations, and the emphasis on negotiations and human rights of the Jimmy Carter administration have all fallen before an overwhelming reliance on military means.

In the context of overall U.S. economic aid to Central America, development has been almost completely subordinated to the logic of military strategy. This trend was convincingly documented in a 1985 congressional report on U.S. aid to El Salvador. Examining a tenfold increase in aid from 1980 through 1984, the investigators found that "direct war-related aid is double the amount of our aid for reform and development; ... the largest single category of aid is indirect war-related economic maintenance, which merely neutralizes the effects of the civil war."[4] The report concludes that "if *all* 'war-related' aid were to be included in one category, it would represent 74 percent of our total aid program."[5]

Second, to a much greater degree than ever before, Washington's policies have been aimed at not just containing radical movements and governments in the Third World, but if possible destroying them. The ultimate goal has been the rollback of socialist experiments. Where that has not been possible, Washington has sought to bleed such experiments economically and militarily until they cease to be attractive alternatives. This is the specific meaning of the "Reagan Doctrine," the claim that the time is ripe to demonstrate to the Soviet Union and its real or imagined Third World allies that "America is resurgent," and that the rules of the superpower rivalry have changed.

From the outset of the Reagan administration, Central America was seen as the most important test case for both the long-standing policy of containment and the newer doctrine of rollback. For both military and political reasons, administration strategists have argued, Central America is the place where the United States can most easily achieve a "victory over communism" and demonstrate that once again, after Vietnam, it was "standing tall." After all, Central America is in the backyard of the United States, traditionally a zone of overwhelming U.S. power and influence. Furthermore, its geographical location is such that the Soviet Union is unlikely to react in vigorous fashion to U.S. initiatives there, especially given Soviet problems with Poland and Afghanistan. In Central America, so the argument has gone, the United States has the home-court advantage. El Salvador thus became the stage for counterinsurgency and containment in action, and Nicaragua the stage for rollback.

Short of all-out war, however, counterinsurgency and rollback are the worst possible antidotes for the development crisis that plagues Central America. The combined strategy assigns a key role to local armed forces (under the correct assumption that there are serious political impediments to introducing U.S. troops in force into the region). Yet even the most superficial familiarity with local history makes it clear that the military has nothing to contribute to the solution of the development crisis. On the contrary, local armies have historically been part of the problem—corrupt, brutal, and reactionary institutions that have been supporters of oligarchic rule, repressors of political movements, and backers of death squads.

The conventional wisdom in Washington has been that the military can be reformed and instructed in winning the "hearts and minds" of the people. To this end, training programs have been an integral part of current policy. But even though such programs—combined with pressure from Washington—may occasionally reduce the murderous brutality of some units, they are irrelevant to the resolution of the development crisis. In fact, continuing close ties with and dependence on the United States tend to strengthen, not weaken, the local armed forces' hold on the levers of power. Thus, despite elections and nominally civilian governments, the military commands in Guatemala, El Salvador, and Honduras remain the ultimate arbiters of most if not all crucial decisions. Washington's current, unstinting support for counterinsurgency and rollback ensures that this will continue to be the case.

The Crucial Choice

The United States faces a crucial choice in Central America: whether to continue the current policy of containment and rollback through endless militarization, or to adopt a policy of diplomacy and demilitarization. The first option implies more killing, destruction, and polarization, runs an ever-increasing risk of full-scale U.S. military involvement, and reduces rather than enhances long-run U.S. and regional security. The second option opens the historic possibility of peace and development leading to a region stabilized not by force of arms, but by international and domestic groups with a shared stake in a newly secure Central America.

Both morally and pragmatically, the second option is the correct choice for the United States. It will not automatically guarantee a stable and prosperous future for the region, but—as the following two chapters make clear—it does stand a substantial chance of advancing democracy, development, and peace.

Proponents of the current policy argue that more time is needed in order for promised results to materialize. Continued economic and military pressure on Nicaragua, they claim, will force the Sandinistas to change their domestic practices and international alliances. Strengthening and modernizing the military in El Salvador will stabilize the situation there, encourage democracy, and eventually allow for the resumption of economic growth. The massive U.S. military buildup in Honduras is justified as only a temporary phenomenon, necessary to ensure that current regional instabilities are not exploited by the Soviet Union and its allies but reversible when the latter "cease their aggression."[6]

Such arguments, so familiar to anyone who remembers official rhetoric about Vietnam, are fundamentally flawed in three ways. First, Central American history gives no evidence that the persistent application of a highly militarized counterinsurgency policy solves the fundamental problems that cause and aggravate the conflict. Second, the overall Central American economic crisis has been exacerbated, not reduced, by current U.S. policies; and the longer these policies continue, the worse the crisis will become, and the more costly and difficult it will be to repair the damage. Third, the Reagan doctrine of rollback, combined with the steady buildup of U.S. military involvement in the region, threatens to escalate into a full-scale war involving massive U.S. intervention. Let us look at each of these issues in turn.

Counterinsurgency

The most continuous and multifaceted counterinsurgency war in the hemisphere has been waged in Guatemala. From 1954 to the present, with determination, considerable sophistication, and fierce brutality, the Guatemalan military has been attempting to stamp out the "subversive threat." Every technique, from scorched earth through "model villages" to "winning hearts and minds," has been tried.

In the course of this war, Guatemala's human rights abuses reached such high levels that foreign aid dried up as a consequence of international revulsion. As a result, the armed forces had no option but to adopt a long-range plan to rid the country of its pariah image. National elections, which would produce a civilian government more acceptable to the international community, were seen as essential. But first, a "final offensive" against "subversion" was designed and implemented from 1981 to 1984.

The generals allowed elections in 1985, and President Vinicio Cerezo took office in 1986. The Guatemalan officers, however, have made it clear to the Cerezo government that they will not tolerate interference in their counterinsurgency programs, nor will they allow fundamental reforms in economic and social institutions. Thus, military dominance of Guatemala continues into its fourth decade, despite the fact that the army's long-term record on the issues of development, democracy, peace, and security has been abysmal.*

The Economic Crisis

Current U.S. policies prolong and deepen the economic crisis of the region. To explore these trends, we have constructed an economic model that generates estimates for growth in the region's economies. Our projections suggest that if current conditions continue, no Central American country will register positive per capita growth between now and 1992.** With a zero-growth economy at best, poverty for most inhabitants of the region will worsen. And even this scenario of stagnation cannot be maintained without very substantial levels of external assistance—estimated at a total of $16.4 billion from 1986 to 1992, or approximately $2.3 billion of external (nonmilitary) financing per year for Costa Rica, Honduras, El Salvador, and Guatemala. Anything less would result in negative rates of per capita growth. Not surprisingly, even with such substantial levels of external financing, regional debt will continue to expand, swelling from $16.3 billion in 1985 to $23.8 billion in 1992. The economic crisis will not end while war continues.

Escalation

The devastation, loss of life, and economic deterioration suffered to date in Central America pale by comparison with what would happen if U.S. military power were used in force in the region. In the case of an invasion and occupation of Nicaragua, for example, the direct economic costs *to the United States* have been estimated at almost $11 billion, and the human cost would include between 2,000 and 5,000 American dead and from 9,000 to 18,000 wounded. Nicaraguan casualties would be

* For more detail, see the Guatemala country report in Part II.
** See Appendix A for details of the economic model and our projections.

31

much higher.[7] Similar losses would be occasioned by an intervention in El Salvador.

Direct intervention would not just involve the invaded country. The Sandinistas and the guerrilla forces in both El Salvador and Guatemala have asserted that should the United States become directly involved with combat troops or air power anyplace in Central America, they would carry the war across borders into neighboring countries. Furthermore, the use of U.S. military power in force would poison U.S. relations with all its strategic allies and trading partners in South America and trigger a moratorium on debt payments. At a minimum, U.S. diplomats, facilities, and businesses throughout the hemisphere would be subject to attacks.

Armed intervention in Central America would also severely strain U.S. relations with Western Europe, Canada, and the Third World. Rather than raising U.S. credibility as an ally who can be trusted, it would suggest more dramatically than has any event in the 1970s and 1980s that the United States is a trigger-happy bully unable to muster sufficient statesmanship to solve problems by diplomacy and negotiations.[8] The U.S. image would be irreparably damaged, much to the advantage of the nation's adversaries.

Given the awesome costs of direct intervention, how could it be regarded as a real possibility? Would any reasonable Washington decision-maker not reject it out-of-hand, on strictly pragmatic grounds? Unfortunately, both past and present actions suggest otherwise.

One key danger derives from the dynamics of U.S. military involvement to date. As Senator Alan Cranston (D, Cal.) has said, "We're talking about a major undeclared war in this hemisphere. This could be a rerun of Vietnam: first American money, then American advisers, then American control of the war, then American troops."[9] The circumstances of Vietnam and Central America are not identical, of course, but the patterns of involvement are similar.[10] Every adviser, every maneuver, every facility constructed, and every American mercenary operating in the region with Washington's "blessings"[11] increases the danger of a war-provoking incident or another decision to up the ante because the previous escalation did not quite do the job. As President Kennedy once remarked after ordering more advisers to Vietnam, "It's like taking a drink. The effect wears off, and you have to take another."[12]

There is a second and perhaps greater danger. What happens if the current U.S. policies of rollback and the destruction of the Sandinistas and the FMLN insurgents fail? What is the next step? If the Reagan administration proves faithful to its announced intentions, at some point massive U.S. intervention becomes the only remaining option. A close observer of American foreign policy has cogently argued that

> the importance of Nicaragua is apparent, for Nicaragua is the litmus test of the Reagan Doctrine. If the promise of the doctrine cannot be realized here, where can it be realized? Nicaragua, then, must not be seen simply, or even primarily as a familiar problem of a great power asserting its control within its traditional sphere of influence. It must instead be seen as something much greater. This is why the administration is so insistent ... that its efforts on behalf of the Nicaraguan rebels cannot be allowed to fail. And this is also why the simple logic of the Administration's commitment in Nicaragua would require it eventually to intervene directly with American forces rather than permit this commitment to fail.[13]

Direct U.S. intervention thus becomes possible not just because existing levels of military involvement risk war-provoking incidents and brinkmanship, and not just because there are relentless and powerful pressures for more advisers, troops, and firepower, but also because the local armies may not be able to do the job that Washington wants them to do. This creates powerful impetus to send in the Marines to do what contras or Salvadoran soldiers have demonstrated that they are incapable of doing on their own.

Notes

[1] *The New York Times*, 18 September 1986.

[2] Quoted in Richard Millett, *Guardians of the Dynasty: A History of the U.S.-Created Guardia Nacional de Nicaragua and the Somoza Family* (Maryknoll, N.Y.: Orbis Books, 1977), 52.

[3] Walter LaFeber, *Inevitable Revolutions: The United States in Central America* (New York: W. W. Norton, 1983), 99.

[4] Rep. Jim Leach (R, Iowa), Rep. George Miller (D, Cal.), and Sen. Mark O. Hatfield (R, Ore.), *U.S. Aid to El Salvador: An Evaluation of the Past, a Proposal for the Future*, report to the Arms Control and Foreign Policy Caucus, February 1985, ii.

[5] Ibid., 14; emphasis in the original.

[6] For an evaluation of Soviet policy and intentions, see C. G. Jacobsen, *Soviet Attitudes Towards, Aid to, and Contacts with Central American Revolutionaries*, prepared in association with R. Jones, Mohiaddin Mesbahi, and Robin Rosenberg for the Department of State, June 1984. See also Cole Blasier, "The Soviet Union," in Morris J. Blachman, William M. LeoGrande, and Kenneth Sharpe, *Confronting Revolution* (New York: Pantheon, 1986), 256–70.

[7] Theodore H. Moran, "The Cost of Alternative U.S. Policies Toward El Salvador, 1984–1989," in Robert S. Leiken, *Central America: Anatomy of Conflict* (New York: Pergamon, 1984), 153–71. For higher estimates, see Lt. Col. John Buchanan, "The Objectives and Costs of U.S. Military Operations Against Nicaragua," *Memo Central America* (Washington, D.C.: Commission on U.S.–Central American Relations, October 1984).

[8] In the words of Jeane Kirkpatrick, "If the opinion that the United States is a reckless gunslinger spreads widely enough, the [NATO] alliance will simply collapse by mutual consent based on distrust on the European side and disgust on the American side." Quoted in Daniel Siegel and Tom Spaulding with Peter Kornbluh, *Outcast Among Allies: The International Costs of Reagan's War Against Nicaragua* (Washington, D.C.: Institute for Policy Studies, November 1985), 18.

[9] *Los Angeles Times*, 16 June 1986.

[10] Between 1964 and 1971, U.S. assistance to South Vietnam increased sixfold. In the seven years beginning in 1979, U.S. assistance to Central America has increased more than tenfold. For U.S. assistance to Central America, see House of Representatives Committee on Appropriations, *Foreign Assistance and Related Programs Appropriations for 1987*, Part I, 731, 740, 749, 758, 767, 785. For U.S. assistance to South Vietnam, see *Congressional Record*, 14 May 1975, S8152. During the same periods, South Vietnamese troop levels more than doubled and the overall size of the four official Central American armies supported by the United States also doubled. For Central American troop levels, see *SIPRI Yearbook 1984* and U.S. State Department, *Challenge to Democracy*, 20. For South Vietnamese troop levels, see Harry G. Summers,

Jr., *Vietnam War Almanac* (New York: Facts on File Publications, 1985). Numbers of U.S. advisers and maneuvers also exhibit similar trends. For Central America, see U.S. Department of Defense, *U.S. Military Strengths–Worldwide* quarterly reports and the *Washington Post*, 18 February 1986, p. A1. For South Vietnam, see Harry G. Summers, op. cit.

[11] Following the downing of the C-123 transport plane carrying arms for the contras in October 1986, Assistant Secretary of State Elliott Abrams said, "I think it's wonderful that Americans, private citizens, are willing to contribute ... but the real heroes of this are those who took risks to get the material delivered." See the *San Francisco Chronicle*, 8 October 1986.

[12] Quoted in "Advisers, Then and Now," *The New York Times*, 24 August 1986.

[13] Robert W. Tucker, "The New Reagan Doctrine Rests on Misplaced Optimism," *The New York Times*, 9 April 1986. Also see Patrick J. Buchanan, "If Not Detente," *National Review*, 30 November 1984.

5

Peace Through Diplomacy

Peace is a daily, a weekly, a monthly process, gradually changing opinions, slowly eroding old barriers, quietly building new structures.

John F. Kennedy, address to the U.N. General Assembly,
20 September 1963

A reversal of the disastrous course now being followed by the United States would put diplomacy and demilitarization at center stage. Progress would not be easy, nor would desired results come quickly. So much blood has been shed, and feelings now run so high, that negotiations leading to demilitarization and then economic regeneration must be seen as a long and difficult *process*. But this is the only process compatible with democracy, development, peace, and long-run security for all concerned.

A Region Demilitarized

What does demilitarization mean in the context of Central America in the late 1980s? Militarization in the region has extended beyond the security sphere into the political, economic, and social fabric of each Central American nation. Therefore, *de*militarization must go beyond mere reductions in armed forces: The relationship between military power and civilian governance must shift in favor of the latter.

Additionally, since militarization is a regional as well as domestic problem, its reversal cannot be accomplished in any one nation in isolation. Demilitarization in Nicaragua, for example, is only possible in the context of demilitarization in Honduras, and demilitarization in Honduras is only possible in the context of demilitarization in El Salvador. Demilitarization must be a complementary process.

It must also be a reciprocal process. With large numbers of foreign advisers and troops present in Central America, the dynamics of the Cold War dictate that "the other side" will respond in kind—in the name of national security, or of aid to a beleaguered ally, or both—to threats, real and imagined. Demilitarization thus means removing Central America from the East-West conflict, or at least from its military and geo-strategic aspects. This, in turn, implies creating a mutually-respected zone of neutrality in Central America. Nicaraguan dependence on Soviet and Cuban military aid cannot be ended without reciprocal reductions of the U.S. military presence in the region. And the U.S. military presence in the region cannot be ended without guarantees that Soviet and Cuban advisers will stay home.

Negotiations, demilitarization, and a zone of neutrality open the way for development and a chance to break the vicious circle of war, economic deterioration, and social disintegration now plaguing the region. Later we will explore how a gradual recovery of economic growth might take shape if accompanied by a reinvigorated structure of trade and bolstered by peacetime levels of savings and investment. Because Central America is a debt-ridden and war-damaged area, significant amounts of foreign loans and aid would still be needed. But unlike the war-time projections presented in the previous chapter, real per capita growth would become possible in a region at peace.

Growth is not, of course, the same as equity-enhancing development. And development, in turn, encourages but does not ensure democratic practices. But unlike the policies now being pursued, development and democracy would have a much better chance if the United States threw its very considerable weight behind negotiations and demilitarization. And if development and democracy had a better chance, so too would real security.

Thus, choosing diplomacy and demilitarization is crucial in a double sense. It enhances short-term security throughout the Americas by bringing the spiral of armed conflict and foreign military involvement in Central America under control. And in the longer term it opens the door to equity-enhancing and stabilizing development—the ultimate guarantee of peace and prosperity in the region.

The Contadora Approach

The United States will inevitably stay involved in Central America, but its involvement must be very different from what it has been thus far. Instead of using its vast resources and military power to impose a made-in-U.S.A. solution on Central America, the United States must use them in the service of diplomacy and the peaceful settlement of disputes. Once this crucial decision has been made, a process of negotiations leading to demilitarization can begin. What might such a process look like? What issues would have to be dealt with? To date, the best answers for these questions have come from the proposals and draft treaties known collectively as Contadora.[1]

The Contadora approach dates from 1983, when representatives of Mexico, Panama, Colombia, and Venezuela met on Contadora Island, off the coast of Panama, and called for a negotiated settlement in Central America. Beginning in 1985, Argentina, Brazil, Peru, and Uruguay formed the Contadora Support Group to throw their weight behind the process. Neither the details of the drawn-out negotiations from 1983 to the present nor the specific outcomes of Contadora are of primary concern here.[2] What is most relevant to us, rather, are the ideas, principles, and mechanisms proposed, which provide an excellent framework for discussing the necessary content and stages of a negotiated settlement.

The basis of Contadora is a proposed treaty among the five Central American nations designed to reduce dramatically the militarization of the area through limitations on and then reductions in arms and troops, both domestic and foreign. Provisions of the treaty call for, in a carefully thought-out set of steps: a modified arms freeze; an arms inventory; a total arms freeze; negotiations to set arms ceilings and limits on military personnel and installations, followed by the reduction of arms and personnel; and the elimination of all foreign military bases and training facilities within six months, along with limitations on foreign advisers. Also called for is an end to all support for irregular military forces—contras, Salvadoran guerrillas, and others. Finally, international military maneuvers would be sharply limited, and verification procedures, including on-site inspection, mandated.

Contadora thus seeks security for the five Central American nations through a negotiated and verifiable process of demilitarization that includes (in fact, is dependent on) the exclusion of foreign bases and personnel from the region, as well as the ending of support for irregular armies. It is a Latin American initiative that says, at least implicitly, that the current crisis in the region has been deepened, not ameliorated, by the actions of foreign powers—in particular, their military policies and practices. In fact, one of the major strengths of the Contadora process is that it seeks regional security through a regional approach, not through the dictates of the Great Powers.

Contadora would thus sharply restrict the policy options available to all foreign powers in Central America. More specifically, although the United States would not formally be a signatory to the treaty, respect for its provisions would effectively terminate the U.S.-sponsored militarization of Honduras, the massive maneuvers currently used to threaten Nicaragua, the presence of U.S. advisers in El Salvador and elsewhere, and—of course—all involvement with the contras. The same rules would apply to the Soviet Union, Cuba, and all other foreign powers.

Can Contadora Work?

A Contadora-type process cannot work unless Washington wants it to, and to date there is little indication that such is the case. In fact, the White House has repeatedly worked through its regional client states, especially Honduras and El Salvador, to delay, draw out, and block the negotiations; pressure has also been applied directly to the Contadora nations.[3] When Nicaragua offered to sign a Contadora draft treaty in September 1984, the administration quickly persuaded other regional governments to reject it. A September 1985 State Department briefing paper to U.S. ambassadors in Central America termed the "collapse" of Contadora preferable to a "bad agreement"— meaning one permitting the continued existence of the Nicaraguan government. As the briefing paper said, "We need to develop an active diplomacy now to head off efforts at Latin solidarity aimed against the U.S. and our allies."[4]

When and if the United States does make the crucial choice in favor of negotiations and demilitarization, however, the Contadora process will still face formidable challenges in Central America itself, foremost among which would be a negotiated settlement in El Salvador and the end of the contra war in Nicaragua. The two cases are dissimilar in many ways, Contadora would affect each differently, and neither will be easy to resolve. In both cases, nevertheless, demilitarization and negotiation hold out hope for an eventual resolution of conflicts that today seem intractable.*

Perhaps the most difficult conflict in Central America is the civil war in El Salvador. The fighting has gone on for so long, political polarization is so profound, and the issues being fought

---

* For more on these topics, see the country reports in Part II.

over are so rooted in a long-standing struggle for land reform and social justice, that the demilitarization of domestic politics and real stability in that troubled country seem a distant dream.

There are reasons for cautious optimism, however. El Salvador, like most of Central America, is a war-weary country. Groups that as little as three or four years ago were intransigent in their opposition to negotiations have softened their positions. Increasingly, the armies on both sides of the conflict have come to realize that a victory in the field is impossible in the foreseeable future, and that some sort of compromise is necessary. All soundings of public opinion reveal overwhelming grass-roots support for negotiations.

Another reason for guarded optimism is the precedent set by Zimbabwe.[5] In 1979, after eight years of civil war in what was then Rhodesia, the Ian Smith government and the black guerrillas were driven to the bargaining table by military stalemate, a crippled economy, and diplomatic pressures from neighboring countries that feared a regionalization of the conflict. Under British auspices, the parties hammered out an agreement that mandated a cease-fire, a new constitution, and plans for one-person-one-vote democracy.

Conditions in Zimbabwe were not identical, of course, to those obtaining in El Salvador today. For example, the British were not militarily involved in the Rhodesian civil war, and the continuation of white minority rule found little support outside of South Africa. Nevertheless, as late as 1978, while the civil war raged in Zimbabwe and feelings were at a fever pitch, few would have predicted that a negotiated solution to the conflict would soon be found. What seems to have been decisive, however, was the pressure of the British government; without it, there would have been no negotiated solution in Rhodesia/ Zimbabwe. If a negotiated settlement is to be found in El Salvador, the U.S. government will have to take an equally constructive role.

The Nicaraguan conflict is fundamentally different from the Salvadoran. An effectively implemented Contadora treaty would greatly reduce the two most important causes of the militarization of Nicaragua: the threat of the contras and the threat of a U.S. invasion. Contadora would guarantee the Sandinista government's right to exist by, in effect, prohibiting attacks by contras based in Honduras and Costa Rica. Moreover, by mandating the withdrawal of Soviet and Cuban military advisers, it would undercut Washington's claims that Nicaragua is being used by Moscow and Havana to threaten Central and North America. In fact, the withdrawal of all foreign military advisers and bases from the region would leave even the most imaginative national security adviser hard-pressed to find any plausible way of presenting Nicaragua as a threat to vital U.S. interests.

Although Contadora would rule out U.S. support for irregular forces, the contras themselves would not automatically or immediately disappear. The demobilization of the contras, their removal from Honduras, and their reincorporation—to the extent possible—into Nicaraguan society would take time, money, and political resolve.

Despite such problems, the basic premise of Contadora remains valid: Security in Central America will come only when arms and troops are reduced, borders are respected, foreign armies and advisers go home, irregular forces are demobilized, and Latin Americans themselves guarantee the sovereignty and integrity of the region. A Contadora treaty will succeed when these principles are accepted—not only by the governments and peoples of the region, but by Washington as well.

Demilitarization and U.S. Security

From the perspective of the most traditional definition of national security—the protection of the territorial integrity of the United States—a Contadora treaty is of marginal importance. The United States has such overwhelming military strength in the hemisphere that no Central American nation ever has been or ever will be a national security threat to the United States.

But a Contadora treaty does directly address several other security concerns of the United States. By barring foreign troops and bases from the region, terminating arms imports, and requiring the eventual withdrawal of military advisers, the treaty would effectively end any possibility of a threatening Soviet or Cuban military presence in Central America. Furthermore, by negotiating reductions in local armed forces, halting outside support for guerrilla groups, and establishing international verification procedures to monitor compliance, Contadora would also ensure that the Nicaraguan revolution could pose no military threat to its neighbors. Thus, an effectively implemented Contadora treaty would respond to the two specific issues most frequently raised in discussions of U.S. security interests in the region.

Security questions, however, extend beyond the military issues addressed by Contadora treaty provisions on troops, arms, bases, and advisers. There is a complex relationship among peace, development, democracy, and security. The Contadora response to this complexity is to bring the overall military situation under control first. Once local military forces have been reduced and the foreign military presence eliminated, the processes of national reconciliation, refugee resettlement, respect for human rights, and development and democracy can occur. In contrast, the standard U.S. response has been: "First we have to get rid of the Soviets, Cuban and (in some versions) the Sandinistas, then we can deal with national reconciliation and all those other things; and finally—after all of that—we can think about the reduction of the U.S. military presence and the local armed forces."[6]

As we have seen, however, the standard U.S. response, no matter how congenial and orderly it might look in the abstract, in practice has meant economic deterioration, political polarization, and human misery in Central America. The 1980s have demonstrated that the regional stability that is properly understood as relevant to the long-run security concerns of the United States *cannot be constructed on the current U.S. policy of militarizing Central America.*

The implications of this fact are far-reaching, in that the United States must give up certain dangerous, long-standing hegemonic assumptions and practices in order to achieve real security in the future. The age of gunboat diplomacy, even when such diplomacy is garbed in modern rhetoric and equipped with the latest weapons, is past. Central America, the United States, and the hemisphere no longer correspond to the old realities.

Contadora is saying to the United States that if it wants peace in Central America, it must relinquish its century-old claim to be the final arbiter of Central America's future and accept a zone of *regional* security guaranteed by Latin America. Contadora is also saying that the United States must trust Latin Americans and international organizations to enforce treaty obligations, even when those treaties bear on legitimate U.S. security concerns. It is promising that in the longer run the United States will be more secure, not less, for having relinquished its self-assumed right to determine—by force of arms if necessary—the kinds of regimes that will be tolerated in the region. Contadora is saying bluntly, "If you want to get something important to you (increased real security in both the short and long run), you must give up the privilege that you have enjoyed for many decades (your military presence and dominance in the region)." The road to security no longer runs through hegemony.[7]

From the outset we have argued that real, long-run security for both Central America and the United States can only be based on the social and political stability that results from a vigorous, participatory, and socially just process of development. Contadora cannot guarantee that outcome; it can only make it more possible and help create the conditions that will give some breathing space to battered economies and beleaguered political systems. Stability-enhancing development will not come easily or quickly. A great deal of residual uncertainty and tension will accompany the process. Surely the

United States can find ways to live with the tension and uncertainty, in the conviction that ending the violence will hasten the day when bread, jobs, and dignity become available for all Central Americans. Until that day, neither Central America nor the United States will be fully secure.

Notes

[1] For Contadora documents, see Bruce M. Bagley, Roberto Alvarez, and Katherine J. Hagedorn, *Contadora and the Central American Peace Process: Selected Documents* (Boulder, Colo.: Westview, 1985).

[2] See "Contadora: Text for Peace," *International Policy Report* (Washington, D.C.: Center for International Policy, November 1984); "Contadora Vows to Continue," *International Policy Report* (Washington, D.C.: Center for International Policy, August 1986); and "Contadora Primer," *International Policy Report* (Washington, D.C.: Center for International Policy, September 1986).

[3] Terry Karl, "Mexico, Venezuela, and the Contadora Initiative," in Morris J. Blachman, William M. LeoGrande, and Kenneth Sharpe, *Confronting Revolution* (New York: Pantheon, 1986), 271–92.

[4] Daniel Siegel and Tom Spaulding with Peter Kornbluh, *Outcast Among Allies: The International Costs of Reagan's War Against Nicaragua* (Washington, D.C.: Institute for Policy Studies, November 1985); and *The New York Times*, 18 August 1985. Reagan administration officials have also sought to turn provisions of the Contadora treaty regarding internal democratization into a weapon against Nicaragua, by urging Honduras, El Salvador, and Costa Rica to insist on language that Managua could not accept. But in a declaration of 12 January 1986, the foreign ministers of the Contadora and Support Group nations reiterated the primary importance of the demilitarization provisions, urging that a treaty entail a simultaneous and immediate freeze on new weapons acquisitions, halt to maneuvers, and cessation of support to irregular forces. They also called on Washington to resume bilateral talks with Nicaragua.

[5] For a good discussion of the Zimbabwe case, see Jeffery Davidow, *A Peace in Southern Africa* (Boulder Colo.: Westview Press, 1984); and Henry Wiseman and Alastair M. Taylor, *From Rhodesia to Zimbabwe* (New York: Pergamon, 1981).

[6] For a useful account of bilateral U.S.-Nicaragua relations, see Roy Gutman, "America's Diplomatic Charade," *Foreign Policy* 56 (Fall 1984): 3–23.

[7] For further exploration of this theme, see Morris J. Blachman, Douglas C. Bennett, William M. LeoGrande, and Kenneth Sharpe, "The Failure of the Hegemonic Strategic Vision" and "Security through Diplomacy: A Policy of Principled Realism," in Blachman, LeoGrande, and Sharpe, op. cit., 329–50 and 351–68.

6

Security Through Development

Peace is an essential condition of economic and social progress.

Kissinger Commission Report, 1984[1]

If a Contadora formula for demilitarization can be implemented in Central America, what are the prospects for development? Almost everyone agrees that the region's economies have significant potential for growth. Central America has good land, underutilized supplies of labor, and a history of very rapid economic growth from 1950 to 1978. But development means more than economic growth. Whereas growth can be measured by increases in gross national product, development can only be measured by improvements in the human condition. Development means enhancing the economic and social well-being of the majority of citizens.

The crucial development challenge is thus to combine economic growth with more-equitable distribution of land, opportunities, and welfare. Equitable distribution was missing from the flawed history of the 1960s and 1970s, and those mistakes must not be repeated if the violence and the destruction of the 1980s are not also to be repeated. Growth without equity—without a fundamental redistribution of assets, benefits, and power—will only set the stage for yet another cycle of conflict. In short, peace is a necessary condition for development, but neither demilitarization nor growth, alone or together, will guarantee the kind of stability-enhancing development essential to the *maintenance* of peace.

The architects of postwar development in Central America will face a formidable set of dilemmas. The 1980s have been a period of global economic crisis, as manifested in the virtual stagnation of growth in world trade and a plunge in the prices of primary commodities. These trends have been devastating for Central America, as well as for other developing countries that depend heavily on commodity exports. Debt has accumulated, capacity to repay has shrunk, unemployment and malnutrition have increased, and forced austerity is almost everywhere the rule.

Moreover, Central America has been tragically scarred by the human and material devastation of almost a decade of conflict. War-related physical damage in El Salvador totals at least $1 billion; in Nicaragua the toll approaches $500 million. Fairly conservative estimates of the cost of repatriating and resettling refugees and displaced persons in the five republics come to another $1.5 billion.[2] The Central American republics cannot absorb these costs unaided. Yet unless these immediate needs are met, development will be even more problematic. A strong case can thus be made that the region will need from $2 to $3 billion in immediate foreign assistance simply to finance essential postwar reconstruction and resettlement.

Beyond reconstruction and resettlement loom fundamental issues of political and economic change. Agrarian reform, programs to meet basic needs, and mechanisms to encourage democratic participation are among the key problems that must be faced if new patterns of development are going to be sustained. Even this short list suggests how potentially divisive the development process inevitably will be—particularly in El Salvador and Guatemala, where military and oligarchical power have traditionally blocked just such reforms. Precisely these demands—for land reform, basic human needs, and democratic participation—forcefully articulated by peasants, workers, the Church, and sectors of the middle class, have been ruthlessly repressed over the past decades. In other words, *real development implies a new and different social pact in which the majority of Central Americans are given voice and eventually opportunities and benefits that they have not traditionally enjoyed*. This new social pact will not be forged with the stroke of a pen. A long, difficult, and conflict-ridden road lies ahead.

The five reports presented in Part II focus in turn on each country involved, emphasizing the specific structural and political problems that each will have to face in order to achieve security and development. The remainder of this chapter introduces some of the general issues that the region and the international community must deal with if the dual challenges of growth and equity are to be met. The list is not exhaustive, and every item does not apply to every country. But taken together, the items listed suggest the profound changes needed to forge a lasting peace in Central America.

Agrarian Reform

Land means both livelihood and power in Central America. Only Nicaragua has instituted an agrarian reform radical enough to break the link between the landed elite and political power—and only after a widely supported popular insurrection put a revolutionary government in power. But revisions in the structure of land ownership are not enough. Questions of credit, productivity, crop diversity, and markets must also be addressed. In El Salvador (admittedly the most difficult case), even if all the arable land were divided into the smallest possible viable individual plots, more than one-third of all peasant families would still have no land. New ways of organizing production to include the landless must be found.

Significant changes in the ownership and use of land raise other crucial questions. Since the economies of Central America will continue to depend heavily on the production, consumption, and export of agricultural products, decisions about who works the land, producing which crops and with what technology, become central in determining everything from foreign exchange earnings to levels of employment and food consumption. It makes a great deal of difference, for example, if the production of staple foods for domestic consumption is given priority over the production of beef cattle for export. In the first case, employment and food self-sufficiency are enhanced; in the second, export earnings are given priority. Rational choices between these options require effective agrarian planning bolstered by realistic price, credit, and tax policies—a pattern rare in the past.

Effective agrarian reform would favor multicrop agriculture aimed at satisfying basic food needs over monocrop export. This pattern of land use offers a much better framework for reducing the excessive use of pesticides and the wanton destruction of the rain forest. For example, intensive use of pesticides on cotton fields in Central America in the 1960s and 1970s led to high levels of pesticide poisoning, as toxins such as DDT accumulated in humans, livestock, and the entire food chain.[3] Also, the expansion of logging and cattle ranching, and the resulting displacement of peasants, are causing some 4,000 square kilometers of Central American rain forest to be destroyed annually.[4] These trends must be reversed.

Industrial Reform

Traditionally, Central American industries have been highly protected by tariffs and oriented to limited sectors of the domestic market. A new development program for the area would expand the industrial sector by concentrating on some mix of agro-industrial production (the processing and refining of agricultural products), export-oriented light industry, and the manufacture of basic consumer goods for expanding domestic and regional markets.

Although in the medium term industry cannot possibly

49

become as important in overall development as agriculture, there is significant room for growth. Equitable development would put increased purchasing power in the hands of people who previously spent little on manufactured goods. A rational development program would attempt to ensure, through an appropriate mix of exchange rates, prices, and taxes, that the majority of this new purchasing power would be spent on goods produced in the region, thus further stimulating local production. Furthermore, since relatively low wages and the proximity to North American markets give a marginal advantage to exports from Central America, growth in manufactured exports is also possible. Some foreign investment will undoubtedly be necessary for exports to expand, but the prospects for an increased inflow of private capital seem reasonably good, provided the region is at peace.[5]

Fiscal Reform

With the partial exception of Costa Rica, Central American countries have very weak fiscal institutions. Tax rates are extremely low and frequently regressive, and evasion and corruption abound. Everywhere budgets run huge deficits, covered (if at all) by the printing of money (as in Nicaragua) or by massive infusions of politically motivated aid from the United States (as in Costa Rica and El Salvador).

At first glance, fiscal reform might appear to be one of the easier aspects of a new development program to implement. With military expenditures declining and the tax base expanding through renewed growth, national balance sheets should improve. Unfortunately, the situation is not so simple. Like agrarian reform, fiscal reform strikes directly at the heart of class-based privilege and traditional political power. To ask the wealthy to pay—whether directly or indirectly—a higher percentage of their income (and wealth) to help finance equity-enhancing development is to ask them to renounce both privilege and power. As the stubborn resistance to the tax reforms proposed by the Duarte government in El Salvador demonstrates, these privileges are rarely given up voluntarily. To date, fiscal reform has been accomplished with some success only in Costa Rica and Nicaragua, the two countries that have undergone significant structural reforms in other areas.

Basic Needs

A development program that neglects basic needs in food, health, housing, employment, and education is doomed to failure. What was possible in the 1950s and 1960s will not be possible in the 1990s. As has been seen since the early 1970s, growth alone cannot lead to social stability unless the living and working conditions of the majority of Central Americans can be improved substantially. Furthermore, few analysts seriously believe that the benefits of growth will "trickle down" to the bottom 60 or 70 percent of the population rapidly enough to meet even their minimal needs and expectations. Thus, for any development program to stand a chance of success in the 1990s, it must incorporate appropriate mechanisms for the delivery of basic goods and services to the majority of the population.

Austerity, however, adds another dimension to this issue. Hard times will be the common lot of most Central Americans in the years immediately ahead, even if programs of economic recovery are quite successful. In times of scarcity, the delivery of minimal levels of goods and services to the majority of the population requires that the well-off also bear a fair share of the burden, through equitable tax policies and other measures. The even-handed distribution of austerity is just as important as the distribution of benefits.

Education

Education is a very long-run investment, and critically important to development. Perhaps no other single indicator tells so much about the depth of the national commitment to both economic growth and the enhancement of equity. In terms of growth, education is properly viewed as investment in human resources. In a country lacking literate and skilled citizens, economic progress will eventually be limited by shortages of trained personnel. On the equity side, vigorous literacy and primary school programs reflect a society's dedication to the advancement of all citizens, rather than just a social or technological elite. One early success of the Nicaraguan revolution was the literacy campaign of 1980. A crowning achievement of the Costa Rican reform movement of 1948 was to develop a system of schools that today has given that country the best educational statistics in the region, and perhaps the highest level of social mobility as well.*

Democratic Participation

Democracy means more than elections. Throughout this century, El Salvador, Guatemala, Honduras, and Nicaragua under the Somozas have held show elections characterized by limited participation and massive fraud. Even elections conducted more honestly, however, do not exhaust the full meaning and substance of democracy.

Democracy means opportunities for ordinary people to choose, organize, and participate, free of fears for their lives and livelihoods. Thus, elimination of repression, encouragement of grass-roots participation, freedom of speech and organization,

* Similar arguments can be made in the public health field, although the economic payoffs of educational programs are more easily measurable.

independence of the judiciary, and civilian control of the military are fundamental to democratic politics. In El Salvador, Guatemala, and Honduras, where the armed forces have long blocked needed reforms, there is little hope of constructing real democracy in the midst of war and continued military domination of politics—no matter how many elections are held.

Furthermore, democracy in its fullest sense is essential to the reform process. Without multiple opportunities for popular participation, changes will neither come fast enough nor go deep enough to ensure that economic benefits flow to the majority and not, as before, to a small minority. Precisely for this reason, democratic participation has always been seen as extremely dangerous—literally subversive—by entrenched elites. The existing structure of privilege cannot survive the full democratization of political life—any more than disproportionate wealth can survive agrarian and fiscal reform.

Regional Trade and Cooperation

The five small republics of Central America can only prosper in the context of vigorous regional trade and cooperation. Despite its shortcomings, the CACM was a stimulus to regional trade in the 1960s and 1970s. With peace, reduced tariffs, and expanding markets, the CACM could be reinvigorated.

More-innovative and long-term regional projects are also required. Central America lacks an integrated system of railroads and a rational structure of ports and shipping facilities. El Salvador, for example, has no access to the Atlantic Coast, and other nations' facilities are duplicative and frequently too small to achieve economies of scale. Building a genuine economic community in the region would require the development of such shared infrastructure. In the beginning, the construction of regional transportation and shipping would be as important in its political symbolism as in its economic potential.

Debt Relief and Foreign Assistance

The Central American debt burden in 1985 was more than $16 billion; if current trends continue, it will reach $19.5 billion by 1988 and $23.8 by 1992 (or more than $900 per capita). In the short run, development and debt repayment simply cannot be made compatible. Thus, debt relief must be an integral part of a development plan for the region. Relief must continue until exports generate surpluses large enough to enable substantial repayments to be made without crippling growth or imposing unacceptable levels of austerity.

Even with debt relief, however, Central America will require large amounts of foreign assistance if acceptable levels of growth are to be achieved and maintained. Estimates of the levels of foreign assistance required range as high as $24 billion (the figure mentioned in the Kissinger report for Central America—including Panama and Belize—for the period 1984–90).[6] Our analysis suggests the need for somewhat lower, but still substantial, levels of external assistance.

In Chapter 4, we estimated that $16.4 billion of additional foreign assistance would be needed by Costa Rica, Honduras, El Salvador, and Guatemala from 1986 to 1992 simply to maintain zero per capita growth under conditions of continuing conflict. Using the same starting point, but changing the assumption to a scenario of peace, we estimate that $15.6 billion in foreign assistance would be needed over the same period for these four countries—*but the consequences for growth would be dramatically different.* In the "peace" scenario, all countries in the region would show healthy per capita growth by 1992 or earlier—with the partial exception of Guatemala, which is likely to take a long time to recover from its mid-1980s slump.*

The fundamental assumption underlying this projection is that a process of demilitarization begins in 1989, leading to a

---

* See Appendix A for details.

gradual increase in exports for the period 1989–92. Coupled with continued restrictions on imports and a gradual return to prewar levels of savings and investment—helped along by a 10 percent internal conversion of military to development spending—the increased exports would lead to a significant recovery of growth in gross domestic product. Debt would increase, but to a lesser amount than under conditions of continuing conflict.

Thus, a scenario based on peace, negotiation, and demilitarization would not only produce much more in the way of growth by 1992, but would actually *cost less* in total foreign assistance, once initial reconstruction costs (noted at the outset of this chapter) have been met. In fact, our analysis understates the potential savings of the peace scenario, since the current foreign assistance figures used do not include U.S. military expenditures in the region. The partial conversion of U.S. regional military expenditures to developmental assistance would substantially reduce the additional funds needed to reach the projected figure of $15.6 billion. Under conditions of negotiated peace, moreover, the possibilities of multiple sources of external funding increase. Foreign governments, banks, businesses, and multilateral lending agencies are more likely to participate in a much-needed foreign aid and investment package if the regional spiral of conflict has been ended.

This sketch of the changes that will have to be made—first to begin and then to sustain an equitable process of development—is daunting. That should not be surprising. The crisis that gave rise to the current conflict was and continues to be profound, and its reversal will require fundamental changes in the economies and societies of the region. It does not follow, however, that the changes or the outcomes will be identical in each country. On the contrary, just as diversity characterizes Central America today, so it will continue to be a fundamental characteristic of the region in the future. A mix of development strategies is needed, desirable, and inevitable.

Similarly, the power to make the necessary changes does not

reside in any one place—not in Washington or in Managua, not in San Salvador, Guatemala City, San Jose, or Tegucigalpa— although each government and each nation must do its part. If there is cause for optimism, in fact, it is precisely because millions of Central Americans in all five countries have increasingly become convinced that the past has not served them well. The United States thus has a double responsibility: first, to step aside and allow Central Americans to determine their own histories and their own futures; and second, as a respectful neighbor, to encourage and support needed changes where possible.

Notes

[1] *The Report of the President's National Bipartisan Commission on Central America*, foreword by Henry A. Kissinger (New York: Macmillan, 1984), 60.

[2] For refugee data and costs, see United Nations High Commissioner for Refugees, *Report on UNHCR Assistance Activities in 1984–85 and Proposed Voluntary Funds Programs and Budget for 1986* (August 1985), 226–58. See also Patricia Ruggles and Michael Fix, *Impacts and Potential Impacts of Central American Migrants on HHS and Related Programs of Assistance* (Washington, D.C.: The Urban Institute, 1985).

[3] Instituto Centroamericano de Investigación y Tecnología Industrial and United Nations Environment Programme, "An Environmental and Economic Study of the Consequences of Pesticide Use in Central American Cotton Production," Guatemala, 1977.

[4] James Nations and Jeffery Leonard, "Grounds of Conflict in Central America," in Andrew Maguire and Janet Welsh Brown, eds., *Bordering on Trouble: Resources and Politics in Latin America* (New York: Adler & Adler, 1986), 55–98.

[5] The case of revolutionary Nicaragua is instructive. Even under the difficult conditions of the 1980s, multinational corporations found that they could invest and operate in Nicaragua. See James E. Austin and John C. Ickis, "Managing After the Revolutionaries Have Won," *Harvard Business Review* 64 (May–June 1986): 103–09.

[6] Of the $24 billion, the report suggests that about half would come from international sources and half from the United States. See *Report of the President's National Bipartisan Commission*, op. cit., 62–63.

PART II
Five Countries, Five Realities

Chapters 1–3 sketched the historic roots of injustice and poverty characteristic of the agro-export economies of Central America and the dismal record of U.S. policy in addressing these problems. Over the last seven years, U.S. policy has not only failed to ease the regional crisis, it has made matters much worse.

The need for alternative polices is therefore pressing, and in Chapters 4 and 5 we outlined a new approach based on negotiation and peace rather than confrontation and war. Our key argument was that only under conditions of peace will development be possible. Finally, Chapter 6 sketched some guidelines for a postwar development strategy.

Part I thus discussed Central America as a region, both because the five countries have much in common, and because current U.S. policy is regional in scope. But our discussion cannot now continue without considering the differences among these countries. Each has a unique history and faces a distinct set of problems, and a thorough understanding of these differences is crucial if we are to grasp the region's dynamics and to formulate viable new policies.*

The main factor these countries have in common is that elites and foreign companies historically have monopolized the best land to grow coffee, bananas, cotton, and other products for export. In general, the result of this process has been the rise to

---

* See Appendix B for country data in tabular form.

power of highly undemocratic governments that regularly violated human rights in order to protect the status quo.

The essential historical differences among these countries lie in the ways they have dealt with pressure from their poor majorities. Costa Rica enjoyed a period of reform in the 1940s, but Guatemala's reforms were utterly undone after the U.S.-organized coup in 1954. In El Salvador and Nicaragua, harsh military rule was established in the 1930s—in El Salvador through a coup and wholesale massacre of rebellious peasants, in Nicaragua through a U.S.-run war against a peasant insurgency. In Honduras, foreign corporations rather than local oligarchs held most of the power; the result was even greater poverty but less internal conflict and violence.

During the 1970s, the region's poor turned increasingly to organization and protest, resulting most dramatically in the Nicaraguan revolution. An expensive U.S.-run counterinsurgency war has helped El Salvador's government survive, while Guatemala's military fought insurgents on their own, with horrifying violence. Nicaragua has been attacked with U.S.-financed guerrilla and economic warfare; Honduras and Costa Rica have been drawn into this war.

Each of the five profiles that follow begins with a brief characterization of the country's current situation and the impact of U.S. policy. Following a historical sketch, we assess the particular difficulties and opportunities the country poses for the formation and carrying out of an alternative policy.

7
Nicaragua

Nicaragua is a country at war. Since 1981 over 20,000 Nicaraguans have been killed and more than 270,000 displaced from their homes. Schools, clinics, houses, and farms have been destroyed and living standards have fallen as the country has suffered at least $2.5 billion worth of damage to its economy—the equivalent of its current annual gross national product.[1]

After more than three decades of intermittent occupation by U.S. Marines, and 46 years of rule by a U.S.-backed dictatorship, Nicaraguans overthrew dictator Anastasio Somoza in 1979. The insurrection, led by the Sandinistas, challenged not only the Central American tradition of rule by the wealthy few, but also the old system that had kept Central America firmly under Washington's control. Some Nicaraguans did not support the revolution, and the process of change since then has been divisive. But the war that plagues Nicaragua is not a civil war—it is a war to preserve its newly-won independence from the United States.

The Reagan administration has organized and financed a contra army whose ultimate goal is to overthrow the Sandinistas and whose interim goal is to damage the Nicaraguan economy and cripple the Sandinista revolution.

History: The Fight for Independence

Nicaragua's experience with foreign intervention began in the 16th century, when the Spanish extracted the country's small mineral wealth and enslaved its indigenous population, forcing many to work in South American mines. Though Nicaragua gained formal independence in 1821, it inherited a colonial elite and remained weak: the British continued to rule the Atlantic Coast (as they had since the 17th century) and the American adventurer William Walker took power briefly in the 1850s.

The coffee boom of the 1880s had the same results in Nicaragua as elsewhere in the region: Large landowners and urban investors expropriated land in the central and northern interior of Nicaragua, leaving many peasants landless and obliged to work on large estates under harsh conditions for little pay.

Nicaraguan President José Santos Zelaya, who took office in 1893, attempted some cautious reforms that were seen as a threat by Washington. After a series of minor interventions the William Taft administration sponsored an insurrection against Zelaya in 1909. With the aid of U.S. Marines and mercenaries, the revolt toppled Zelaya, and a pro-U.S. government was installed in 1910.[2] The Marines returned in 1912 to crush a revolt against this government, stayed until 1925, and then returned the following year to battle the guerrilla army of Augusto César Sandino. They did not finally leave until 1933.

Anastasio Somoza García, the leader of the Nicaraguan National Guard established by the United States as it pulled its troops out of the country, tricked Sandino into negotiating peace and then had him killed in 1934. The next day, the National Guard massacred Sandino's troops and their families around the northern mountain town of Wiwilí, where they had established agricultural cooperatives in the "peace" agreed to by Somoza.

The Somoza dynasty—Somoza García died in 1956 and was succeeded by his eldest son, Luís Somoza Debayle, who was followed by the younger son, Anastasio Somoza Debayle, in 1967—became immensely wealthy, powerful, and corrupt.[3] The Somozas eventually came to own or control a large share of the nation's productive resources, including one-third of the arable land and many major industries.[4] The Somoza-led Nicaraguan National Guard was a central feature of the family's rule.[5]

Just before Christmas 1972, an earthquake destroyed most of downtown Managua. Millions of dollars flowed to Nicaragua to help the victims, but the Somozas and their cronies diverted much of it to themselves. Anti-Somoza feeling increased dramatically as a result.

While political parties and labor unions tried to challenge Somoza's political power, the *Frente Sandinista de Liberación Nacional* (FSLN), founded in 1961, sought to dislodge the dictatorship by force. As the FSLN grew stronger after 1972 and carried out several daring attacks, Somoza unleashed a wave of repression that, combined with his corruption, alienated and brought most Nicaraguans together against the dictatorship.[6] This political struggle came to a head during 1978, as escalating protest and revolt were answered by indiscriminate violence from the National Guard.

Mexico, Venezuela, Panama, Costa Rica, Cuba, and many European nations all actively opposed the dictator, although the United States did not withdraw its support for Somoza until just before he fell.[7]

The FSLN, backed by a popular insurrection, achieved a military victory in July 1979. Somoza looted the country's treasury before he fled, leaving behind only $3.5 million and a $1.6 billion foreign debt.

The FSLN-led coalition that brought down Somoza was very broadly based, spear-headed by young people. (In Nicaragua over half the population is under 20 years of age.) The participation of peasants, workers, and the urban poor was vital.[8] Also involved were the majority of intellectuals, professionals, church people, as well as a substantial number of businessmen who opposed the avaricious practices of the Somozas.

Since 1979 Nicaragua has undergone a profound process of social change aimed at responding to the needs of the poor majority. This process of change has not always gone smoothly, and many who were relatively well-off under Somoza have felt their positions threatened. Thus it is not surprising that the broad coalition of those opposed to Somoza did not endure once the dictator was gone. The Sandinista Front has prevailed in the postrevolutionary era not only because the FSLN was primarily responsible for the overthrow of Somoza, but also because its program, although beset with difficulties, continues to hold out the hope of significant improvements in the welfare of the poor majority.

The Role of the Church

In the late 1970s Nicaragua's Christian churches began to denounce the injustices perpetrated by the Somozas, and became engaged in the struggle against the dictatorship. In June 1979 the Roman Catholic bishops declared that conditions existed for a legitimate armed insurrection. In November 1979, they recognized the role of the FSLN in leading the revolutionary process, discussed the compatibility of socialism and Christianity, and declared the new situation in Nicaragua a privileged opportunity for the Roman Catholic Church to carry out its preferential option for the poor. In 1980 the FSLN acknowledged the positive role of religious faith and institutions in motivating people to fight for justice and stated its commitment to freedom of religion.

The revolution deepened political divisions within the Catholic Church that dated from the 1970s, when many priests, nuns, and lay missionaries began working directly with the poor, laying the basis for the "church of the poor" that actively supported the FSLN.[9] After 1980, more-conservative bishops and clergy began to view this grass-roots church as too supportive of the Sandinistas and a challenge to the bishops' authority. A series of incidents, including Pope John Paul II's controversial visit in 1983, increased friction. Several prominent clergymen became outspokenly critical of the government's policies, refused to condemn contra attacks on civilians, and even hinted at support for the contras. Because of the war, tensions between the Catholic hierarchy and the Nicaraguan government heightened to the point where several priests and a bishop were expelled from the country. Since September 1986, relations have improved modestly, and some serious dialogue has occurred. A newly appointed Papal Nuncio has been instrumental in this process.

Nicaragua has a variety of Protestant denominations. It is estimated that the number of Protestants has doubled since 1979, to roughly 15 percent of the population. Much of the increase has come among Pentecostals who in general are not supportive of the present government. Other Protestants such as the Baptist Convention, however, are involved in health and other development projects that coincide with the government's social goals. Currently, there are approximately 2,000 Protestant ministers in the country, compared to 1,500 in 1979. The Catholic church has also grown institutionally since 1979, with the number of parishes increasing from 167 to 178, of priests from 293 to 430, and of seminaries from two to eight. Denominational schools, both Catholic and Protestant, receive substantial state subsidies.

United States Policy

The Reagan administration came to power in 1981 publicly committed to getting rid of the Sandinista government[10] and immediately leveled a barrage of accusations against Nicaragua:[11]

- Although Soviet trade with and aid for Nicaragua was minimal (and Peru had a vastly greater arsenal of Soviet weaponry, including advanced aircraft), the Reagan administration characterized the receipt of arms from the Soviet Union as threatening to Nicaragua's neighbors.[12]
- Although Nicaragua had four priests in the government, the administration depicted the Sandinista revolution as atheistic and hostile to religion.
- Although 60 percent of the Nicaraguan economy remained (and remains) in private hands, the administration described the country as communist.[13]
- Although no solid evidence of Nicaraguan government complicity in arms smuggling to the Salvadoran insurgents, or even of any arms shipments coming through Nicaraguan territory after early 1981, was ever presented, the Sandinistas were repeatedly accused of subverting El Salvador.

In 1981 the Reagan administration began to organize and supply elements of Somoza's National Guard who had fled into Honduras after the revolution.[14] U.S. policy also sought to exploit suspicion of the Sandinistas among Indian groups on the country's isolated Atlantic Coast by arming hostile Miskito Indian bands there.

Although the contras have never succeeded in holding any significant territory or towns, in 1983 and 1984 they did inflict heavy casualties. Contra operations have typically been characterized by attacks on civilian targets, especially agricultural cooperatives, schools, and clinics, and on the murder of teachers, doctors, agricultural technicians, and anyone else associated with government programs.[15]

In late 1983 the Nicaraguan government established compulsory military service, a policy that generated considerable controversy within the country. During 1985 and 1986 the army, now larger, better-trained, and better-equipped, put the contras on the defensive. Citizens' militias have also played an important role in national defense; by

1986 some 200,000 weapons had been distributed to the population.

The contras have not managed to develop a significant popular base in the country.[16] Although they have attracted several thousand disaffected Nicaraguans to their ranks, their military command has been drawn almost entirely from Somoza's National Guard.[17]

The Atlantic Coast

The Atlantic Coast was colonized by the British and influenced by Moravian (Protestant) missionaries. Although nominally part of Nicaragua, the coast was always more Caribbean than Latin, had little contact with the western two-thirds of the country, and was not drawn into the struggle against Somoza. When the Sandinistas sought to administer the region after their victory and to implement economic and social reforms, they were met with suspicion and hostility. After U.S.-armed Miskito Indian groups based in Honduras staged attacks in the Rio Coco border area at the end of 1981, the government relocated inhabitants inland. Contra attacks escalated, and several human rights violations by Sandinista forces, as well as by armed Miskito groups, took place between 1981 and 1984.[18]

Since 1984 the Sandinistas have publicly acknowledged their errors. Recognizing demands for a degree of autonomy in the multiethnic Atlantic Coast, they opened talks with willing representatives of armed groups that resulted in a general ceasefire by mid-1985.[19] Inhabitants of the Rio Coco area were allowed to return, and an extensive consultation process was undertaken with the population on issues of autonomy. The new Nicaraguan constitution guarantees respect of the coast's cultural and linguistic diversity, allows bilingual education, upholds traditional patterns of land tenure and resource use, encourages appropriate economic development, and promises the creation of an autonomous regional government. Progress on the autonomy issue has been significant among the blacks and mestizos who make up the majority on the Atlantic Coast, but serious issues remain to be resolved, particularly with the Miskito Indians.

From Development to a Wartime Economy

Nicaragua maintained the highest rate of economic growth, and the highest rate of investment of any country in Latin America, between 1979 and 1983.[20] In the years after the revolution, infant mortality was reduced from 120 to 70 deaths per 1,000 live births, polio was virtually eradicated, and the proportion of illiterate citizens was reduced from 53 to 12 percent.

These facts help explain why U.S. efforts to blame the Sandinistas for later economic difficulties have had so little impact inside Nicaragua, and why a majority of the population sees the U.S. war against Nicaragua as the primary source of its problems. Nicaraguans, especially the poor, experienced a marked improvement in their living standards during the first years of the Sandinista revolution, before the war reached a destructive level.[21]

After 1983 the intensifying war provoked a negative rate of growth, a drastic reduction in the rate of investment, and large cuts in health and education services—a painful shift from reconstruction to a wartime economy.[22] Money for long-term investment was rechanneled to defense and to guaranteeing basic food for the population. Survival, not growth, became the priority.

Nicaragua has had to find new trading partners and new sources of foreign aid to counteract Washington's punitive economic measures. Soon after coming to power the Reagan administration cut off bilateral economic aid. Donations from the Soviet Union, Greece, Canada, Sweden, East Germany, France, Argentina, and other countries have helped meet the demand for wheat and other foodstuffs. In 1982 the Reagan administration reduced Nicaragua's annual sugar export quota by 90 percent. The United States also has intervened to deny Nicaragua several loans from multilateral institutions, particularly the Inter-American Development Bank.[23] When President Reagan embargoed U.S. trade with Nicaragua in May 1985, that trade had already fallen to half its 1979 level.[24]

Pressure on Mexico to stop selling oil to Nicaragua forced a frantic search for new petroleum sources and a trip to the Soviet Union by President Daniel Ortega in May 1985. Defense needs have also been met by arms shipments from the Soviet Union and Eastern bloc nations.

The State of Emergency: Political Restrictions

As contra attacks increased, the Nicaraguan government declared a state of emergency in 1982, imposing prior censorship of the press, restrictions on outdoor political rallies, and detention without trial in cases of involvement with the counterrevolution. In 1986, under the state of emergency, the newspaper *La Prensa* was shut down after it received funds from a U.S.-sponsored organization and its editor publicly supported U.S. aid to the contras in a 3 April 1986 article in the *Washington Post*. Calling *La Prensa* "an American newspaper published in Nicaragua," the government announced its indefinite suspension on 26 June 1986, the day after the United States House of Representatives voted to supply the contras with $100 million.

Nicaragua's state of emergency, though serious and clearly restrictive, should, however, be distinguished from the states of siege and other measures imposed in recent years in Guatemala and El Salvador, which have included curfews, extensive restrictions on meeting and movement, widespread detentions, and suppression of all opposition political activity, backed up by disappearances, torture, and assassination by security forces and military-sponsored death-squads.

The Nicaraguan government has repeatedly committed itself

to lifting the state of emergency as soon as the contra war ceases. An amnesty is currently in effect for the contras and refugees. Over 2,000 contras are reported to have taken advantage of the amnesty, and some 10,000 Miskitos returned to Nicaragua in early 1987.

Political Activity

Elections were held in November 1984. Three-quarters of the eligible voters participated, and the FSLN won 67 percent of the popular vote.[25] For the 1984 election the FSLN offered as its platform the same principles that it had originally put forward in 1979, and that form the basis for the constitution adopted in January 1987 after a two-year process of national and international consultation:

1. *A mixed economy with public, private, and cooperative sectors.* In 1985 the public sector accounted for 40 percent of the gross domestic product, and the private and cooperative sectors for 30 percent each.
2. *Political pluralism.* Seven political parties, ranging in ideology from communist to conservative, took part in the 1984 election and the subsequent process of writing a new constitution. Another seven parties that chose not to participate in the elections remain active.
3. *Nonalignment with either the East or West and diversified economic relations.* Until the U.S. embargo in May 1985, roughly 20 percent of Nicaragua's trade was with the United States, 40 percent with other Western countries, 30 percent with the Eastern bloc, and 10 percent with other nonaligned countries.[26]
4. *Participatory democracy based on programs that favor a majority of citizens.*[27] The Council of State, comprised of representatives from various sectors and interest groups, was succeeded by a National Assembly elected in 1984.

The new constitution, debated in public forums and then written with the participation of all seven parties in the Nicaraguan assembly, provides broad guarantees of civil liberties. The government has already granted greater political autonomy to the peasant organization UNAG and to neighborhood organizations.

The Nicaraguan government began granting individual land titles to peasants in 1984, and two years later announced that the province of Río San Juan in the south was the "first territory free of landless peasants." Whereas large landowners controlled 36 percent of the arable land in 1978, in 1985 they retained only 11 percent.[28] Participation in cooperatives is encouraged through favorable credit arrangements but is not required as a condition for receiving land.

Diplomacy

For the Nicaraguan government, the achievement of its social agenda depends on the securing of peace. Although the government views the war as the result of U.S. policy toward Nicaragua, other countries in the region have been drawn in. Thus, Nicaragua has proposed a series of steps toward a regional settlement that would also address hemispheric security concerns:

1. The prohibition of foreign military bases and the limitation of maneuvers and advisers.
2. Mutual reductions in offensive military equipment in a regional disarmament process.
3. The demilitarization of borders, acceptance of multilateral peacekeeping forces, and the conversion of Central America into a demilitarized zone under the auspices of Contadora, the Lima Group, and the United Nations.
4. Effective mechanisms of on-site verification and control.

Prospects for a New Policy

The United States must first of all stop its war against Nicaragua. This policy not only has been destructive to Nicaragua, but also stands as the key obstacle to reaching a peace settlement in Central America. A new U.S. policy must respect Nicaraguan sovereignty, while understanding the country's nationalism and its long fight for independence.

For Nicaragua, an alternative U.S. policy would end the contra war and allow a process of national reconstruction to resume. Without the war polarizing the country's political life, the government should be able to lift restrictions on political activity, and the conservative opposition might then be prepared to work peacefully within the political process. A new U.S. policy based on mutual respect of course should include a strong human rights component. But under the current conditions, in which Washington sponsors a terrorist force responsible for gross human rights violations within Nicaragua, U.S. demands for an easing of internal restrictions lack both efficacy and moral force.

A new U.S. policy also offers the opportunity of rebuilding trade, aid, and other economic relations. Nicaragua's mixed economy is an important source of resilience and diversity and should be encouraged: U.S. aid should not be conditioned on rigid adherence to free market orthodoxy. Lifting the trade embargo would benefit both countries.

Finally, a new policy must address the residue of suspicion and ill-feeling inevitable after years of war. Fortunately, thousands of U.S. citizens have already begun carrying out an alternative policy toward Nicaragua. They have contributed time and expertise, helped build schools and pick coffee, raised money for medical supplies, and even traveled to border areas in hopes of discouraging contra raids. This work has laid the basis for a policy of reconciliation.

Notes

[1] This figure includes not only direct physical damage caused by contra assaults but also indirect costs caused by the dislocations of the war. See E. V. K. Fitzgerald, "An Evaluation of the Economic Costs of U.S. Aggression Against Nicaragua," in Rose J. Spalding, ed., *The Political Economy of Revolutionary Nicaragua* (Boston: Allen & Unwin, 1987); United Nations Economic Commission for Latin America, *Notas para el estudio económico de América Latina y el Caribe, 1984: Nicaragua* (Mexico: 17 April 1985); and Raúl Vergara, et al., *Nicaragua: país sitiado, Cuadernos de Pensamiento Propio*, Serie Avances No. 4 (Managua: CRIES, June 1986).

[2] Thomas Walker, *Nicaragua: The Land of Sandino* (Boulder, Colo.: Westview, 1986), 15–19.

[3] John A. Booth, *The End and the Beginning: The Nicaraguan Revolution* (Boulder, Colo.: Westview, 1982).

[4] Gregorio Selser, *Nicaragua de Walker a Somoza* (México: Editorial Mex Sur, 1984), 273–99.

[5] Richard Millett, *Guardians of the Dynasty: A History of the U.S.-Created Guardia Nacional de Nicaragua and the Somoza Family* (Maryknoll, N.Y.: Orbis, 1977); and Walter LaFeber, *Inevitable Revolutions: The United States in Central America* (New York: W. W. Norton, 1984).

[6] Organization of American States, Inter-American Commission on Human Rights, *Report on the Situation of Human Rights in Nicaragua*, 17 November 1978.

[7] U.S. aid and support for Somoza continued until the fall of 1978. In the following months, President Jimmy Carter sought to jettison Somoza while using military force to block the Sandinistas and bring to power another U.S.-aligned government. The effort was blocked by the Organization of American States, which denounced Carter's proposed "peacekeeping force" as U.S. interference. Carter continued to press for a settlement that would preserve Somoza's National Guard as part of the country's postrevolutionary police and military. After the Sandinista victory, the Carter administration established reasonably good relations with the new government. See Richard R. Fagen, "Dateline Nicaragua: The End of the Affair," *Foreign Policy* 36 (Fall 1979): 78–91; William M. LeoGrande, "The Revolution in Nicaragua: Another Cuba?" *Foreign Affairs* 58 (Fall 1979): 28–50; and Dennis Gilbert, "Nicaragua," in Morris J. Blachman, William M. LeoGrande, and Kenneth Sharpe, eds., *Confronting Revolution* (New York: Pantheon, 1986), 88–124.

[8] Carlos M. Vilas, *The Sandinista Revolution: National Liberation and Social Transformation in Central America* (New York: Monthly Review Press, 1986).

[9] On background to the doctrinal shifts in the Church, see Penny Lernoux, *Cry of the People* (Garden City, N.Y.: Doubleday, 1980), 11–38.

[10] The 1980 Republican Party platform stated: "We deplore the Marxist Sandinista takeover of Nicaragua. . . . We will support the efforts of the Nicaraguan people to establish a free and independent government." For views of

other incoming administration officials, see Jeane Kirkpatrick, "U.S. Security and Latin America," *Commentary* 71 (January 1981): 29–40 and Constantine Menges, "Central America and its Enemies," *Commentary* 72 (August 1981): 32–38. See also Joanne Omang, "Rebel Fund Diversion Rooted in Early Policy," *Washington Post*, 1 January 1987.

[11] A useful compilation of administration falsehoods can be found in *In Contempt of Congress: The Reagan Record of Deceit and Illegality on Central America* (Washington, D.C.: Institute for Policy Studies, 1985; rev. version, 1987).

[12] When Nicaragua bought some arms from France, the Reagan Administration continued to push the Soviet-arms-shipments line and pressured the French to stop the sales. See Robert Matthews, "The Limits of Friendship: Nicaragua and the West," *NACLA Report on the Americas* 19 (May–June 1985): 22–32. According to leaked CIA reports, Soviet arms supplied to Nicaragua have been of a defensive character, and the supplies did not become significant until after the United States stepped up aid to the contras; see Clifford Kraus and Robert Greenberger, "Despite Fears of U.S., Soviet Aid to Nicaragua Appears to be Limited," *Wall Street Journal*, 3 April 1985; and Joel Brinkley, "Nicaraguan Army: 'War Machine' or Defender of a Besieged Nation?" *The New York Times*, 30 March 1985. See also Dennis Gilbert, "Nicaragua," in Morris J. Blachman, LeoGrande, and Sharpe, op. cit.; and Colin Danby, et al., *The Military Balance in Central America: An Analysis and Critical Evaluation of Administration Claims* (Washington, D.C.: Council on Hemispheric Affairs, 5 April 1985).

[13] A balanced view of Sandinista domestic and foreign policies can be found in Thomas W. Walker, ed., *Nicaragua: The First Five Years* (New York: Praeger, 1985).

[14] *The Tower Commission Report* (New York: Bantam Books, 1987), 450.

[15] Recent claims by contra forces that efforts are being made to improve human rights practices have not been borne out by results. See Americas Watch, *Human Rights in Nicaragua: 1985–1986* (Washington, D.C.: Americas Watch, 1986).

[16] Former U.S. SOUTHCOM Commander General Paul Gorman characterized the contras in February 1987 as "a cross-border raiding force." George C. Wilson, "Contras Need a Success Soon, Crowe Says," *Washington Post*, 13 February 1987.

[17] A study by the Arms Control and Foreign Policy Caucus of the U.S. Congress found that 46 of the 48 key contra military commanders at the time, from Commander Enrique Bermúdez on down, had been in the National Guard; these included Chino Lau, who is reported to have played a key role in the 1980 murder of Oscar Romero, the Archbishop of San Salvador. See Arms Control and Foreign Policy Caucus, *Who Are the Contras? An Analysis of the Makeup of the Leadership of the Rebel Forces, and the Nature of the Private American Groups Providing Them Financial and Material Support* (Washington, D.C.: 18 April 1985).

[18] Americas Watch has issued a number of key documents on the human

rights situation in the Atlantic Coast. See especially *Human Rights in Nicaragua: Reagan, Rhetoric, and Reality* (July 1985), which notes that of the two most serious incidents attributed to Nicaraguan forces, "there is no evidence that they were directed or condoned by the central government. . . . There has never been any evidence of racially-motivated or widespread killing of Miskitos." See also *Violations of the Laws of War by Both Sides in Nicaragua, 1981–1985* (1985) and *Miskitos in Nicaragua: 1981–1984* (1984). Another important document is *Trabil Nani: Historical Background and Current Situation on the Atlantic Coast of Nicaragua*, issued by the Center for Research and Documentation of the Atlantic Coast and the Riverside Church Disarmament Project. See also Martin Diskin, et al., "Peace and Autonomy on the Atlantic Coast of Nicaragua: A Report of the LASA Task Force on Human Rights and Academic Freedom," *LASA Forum* 16 (Spring 1986) and *LASA Forum* 17 (Summer 1986).

[19] "The Atlantic Coast: War or Peace," *Envío* 4 (October 1985): 1c–13c.

[20] See Michael E. Conroy, "Economic Legacy and Policies: Performance and Critique," in Thomas W. Walker, ed., *Nicaragua: The First Five Years* (New York: Praeger, 1985), 219–44.

[21] See ibid. Also see Richard R. Fagen, *The Nicaraguan Revolution: A Personal Report* (Washington, D.C.: Institute for Policy Studies, 1981).

[22] These shifts in economic policy are discussed in Roberto Pizarro, "The New Economic Policy: A Necessary Readjustment," in Rose J. Spalding, ed., *The Political Economy of Revolutionary Nicaragua* (Boston: Allen & Unwin, 1987), 217–32. See also Central American Historical Institute, "Slow Motion Toward a Survival Economy," *Envío* 5 (September 1986): 13–38.

[23] Jim Morrell and William Jesse Biddle, *Central America: The Financial War* (Washington, D.C.: Center for International Policy, 1983); and "U.S. Economic Measures Against Nicaragua," *Update, Central American Historical Institute* 4 (1 April 1985): 1–4.

[24] Michael E. Conroy, "Patterns of Changing External Trade in Revolutionary Nicaragua: Voluntary and Involuntary Trade Diversification," in Rose J. Spalding, op. cit., 169–94.

[25] Former West German Social Democratic leader Willy Brandt, who took a major role in preparations leading up to the elections, praised them and disparaged those who, under U.S. prodding, failed to take part. For other comments on the elections, see Latin American Studies Association (LASA), *The Electoral Process in Nicaragua: Domestic and International Influences*, Report of the LASA Delegation to Observe the Nicaraguan General Election of November 4, 1984 (Austin, Texas: 19 November 1984); and International Human Rights Law Group and Washington Office on Latin America, *A Political Opening in Nicaragua: Report on the Nicaraguan Elections of November 4, 1984* (Washington, D.C.: December 1984).

[26] See Central American Historical Institute, "U.S. Allies Continue Aid and Trade Relations With Nicaragua," *Update* 5 (27 February 1986): 1–7.

[27] For an exploration of revolution, participation, and democracy in Nicaragua, see Peter Marchetti's "War, Popular Participation, and Transition

to Socialism" in Richard R. Fagen, Carmen Diana Deere, and José Luís Coraggio, eds., *Transition and Development: Problems of Third World Socialism* (New York: Monthly Review Press, 1986), 303–30.

[28] Joseph Collins, et al., *Nicaragua: What Difference Could a Revolution Make?*, 2nd ed. (San Francisco: Institute for Food and Development Policy, 1985); and Carmen Diana Deere, et al., "The Peasantry and the Development of Sandinista Agrarian Policy, 1979–1984," *Latin American Research Review* 20 (1985): 75–109.

8
El Salvador

For more than seven years the military-dominated government of El Salvador, with heavy backing from the United States, has been fighting against a guerrilla insurgency. The war has left over 60,000 dead out of a population of 5 million, more than 1.2 million refugees and displaced people, and over $1 billion in damage to homes, crops, and infrastructure.[1]

With massive infusions of U.S. aid, the economy has recovered slightly in recent years, but it is still operating at only 80 percent of 1978 levels. Real wages have fallen 60 percent, and more than two-thirds of the work force is unemployed or underemployed. Once proud of its reputation as the "Hong Kong of the New World," El Salvador now depends for its economic survival on U.S. aid and family remittances from abroad.[2]

As the Salvadoran government becomes more and more dependent on the United States for economic survival, the fundamental problems of inequity and repression, which sparked the insurgency, are as far as ever from being addressed. And although U.S. training and equipment have strengthened the Salvadoran armed forces, they have not turned the tide in the war. The initiative has shifted back and forth, but the insurgents still have the capacity to fight throughout the country, disrupt the economy, and stage devastating surprise attacks.

A History of Inequity

El Salvador's civil war is rooted in its highly inequitable distribution of land. Because a small elite, or oligarchy, owns most of the land, the vast majority of the rural population has either been relegated to a marginal agrarian existence or forced to join the growing numbers of landless laborers. Beginning 100 years ago, when laws were enacted permitting the seizure of communal holdings, the peasant population of El Salvador has been repeatedly and systematically pushed off the best agricultural land; when they have tried to resist, they have been repressed. By enforcing these injustices for the oligarchy, the military gained increasing political power for itself.

In 1931 a reformist named Arturo Araujo was elected president. The army promptly overthrew him. When peasants in the western part of the country revolted in January 1932, the military put down the uprising and, over a period of several weeks, systematically massacred an estimated 30,000 peasants.[3] This atrocity, still known simply as *la matanza* (the massacre), marked the full assumption of political power by the Salvadoran armed forces. Although different military factions have periodically overthrown each other, the army has proven a remarkably durable political institution, holding effective power to this day.

In the 1950s and 1960s even more peasants were pushed off their lands, not only in the coffee-growing highlands but also along the coastal plains where traditional sharecroppers were evicted, by the boom in cotton.[4] By the end of the 1970s, at least 60 percent of rural families had either no land at all or less than subsistence plots.[5] El Salvador's 1971 census showed that 64 percent of the land belonged to 4 percent of the country's farms. Although the agricultural export sector generated high demand for rural labor at planting and harvest time, low prevailing wages condemned the landless to abject poverty. Many migrated to nearby Honduras or to urban areas in search of employment.

Despite a rapidly growing manufacturing sector, stimulated first by the Central American Common Market and then by the creation of a duty-free zone for garment and electronics assembly plants, joblessness had already reached crisis proportions before the outbreak of the civil war. Thus, despite the nation's impressive aggregate growth rates in the post-World War II period, the majority of Salvadorans failed to benefit. During the 1970s, income distribution actually worsened.

Vigorous union activity began in the 1920s but was suppressed after 1932. It reemerged in the 1950s and gained a measure of tolerance in the 1960s. Peasant organizations, however, have generally been prohibited and harshly repressed.[6] Peasant organizers were particularly hard-hit in the early 1980s.

Opposition

During the 1960s, some opposition political parties were permitted to compete with the official military party for municipal and national offices. The Christian Democratic Party became the principal opposition group during this period, growing from a small, conservative party into a strong national organization rooted in the cities and larger towns.[7] In the early 1970s the Christian Democrats began to back land reform, and for the 1972 presidential election they entered into an alliance with the social democratic National Revolutionary Movement (MNR) and the National Democratic Union (UDN), a front for the outlawed Communist Party. The coalition's presidential candidate was the Christian Democratic mayor of San Salvador, José Napoleón Duarte; its vice-presidential candidate was MNR head Guillermo Ungo.

When this slate won, the military canceled the results and installed the candidates of the official party. By blocking the electoral road to change, the military laid the basis for the armed revolution of the 1980s.

During the 1970s, mass organizations expanded and became

77

important in El Salvador—as they did throughout the region—incorporating peasants, workers, students, slum dwellers, and some professionals, such as teachers. The pastoral work of El Salvador's Catholic Church played an indirect but important role in this political awakening. Encouraged by the Church's identification with the poor and its critique of injustice and poverty, priests, nuns, and lay workers organized Christian base communities, trained catechists, and ultimately helped peasants resist the depredations of large landowners.

The violent response by the landlords and the military pushed even conservatives in the Church hierarchy to take a position of stronger protest and opposition. The murder in 1977 of rural pastor Father Rutilio Grande marked an important turning point. San Salvador's new archbishop, Oscar Romero, became increasingly outspoken in denouncing the repression.

The success of the Nicaraguan revolution in July 1979 encouraged the popular movement as much as it alarmed the Salvadoran army, the oligarchy, and the Carter administration. With protest and repression in El Salvador escalating in 1979, junior officers overthrew the government of General Carlos Humberto Romero in October 1979 and installed a provisional junta that incorporated progressive civilians, among them Guillermo Ungo, and pledged to make an opening to the left, investigate human rights abuses, and implement land reform.

But power remained with rightist officers in the armed forces, who organized the most sweeping campaign of repression since the *matanza* of 1932. In the period 1977–79 a strong underground movement had been organized in the cities, capable of mobilizing hundreds of thousands. The military's aim was not only physically to eliminate this popular organization, but also, as in 1932, to create a climate of terror so intense that no new movement would grow. In 1980–81 the security forces, often operating at night and in civilian clothes as "death squads," sought out and killed more than 21,000 civilians.[8] Anyone even suspected of leftist sympathies was a target; victims included unionists, teachers, religious workers, students, and health workers.[9]

The progressive civilians in the October junta resigned at the end of 1979 in despair at their inability to stop the killings. A new junta, formed with several Christian Democrats, collapsed in March 1980, in part because of the death-squad murder of Christian Democratic attorney general Mario Zamora. Finally, the only prominent civilian politician that the military could find to join and stay in the junta was José Napoleón Duarte. Two weeks after Duarte joined the junta, Archbishop Oscar Romero was assassinated while saying mass. Duarte was named president of the junta in December 1980 and served in that capacity until March 1982.

The Insurgency Begins

The Democratic Revolutionary Front (FDR), formed in April 1980, included popular and peasant organizations, unions and professional groups, Ungo's MNR, and dissident Christian Democrats. It, in turn, allied itself with the coalition of insurgent organizations to present a united opposition. But overtures to negotiate were ignored by the government, and in November 1980 the FDR's five principal leaders, including its president, former agriculture minister Enrique Alvarez, were abducted from a meeting by death-squad members as the Treasury Police secured the area. All five were tortured and killed.

The guerrilla Farabundo Martí Front for National Liberation (FMLN—named after one of the leaders of the 1932 revolt) stepped up its activities in January 1981. The outgoing Carter administration, which had suspended lethal military aid on human rights grounds, reluctantly restored the aid, a precedent enthusiastically followed by the Reagan administration. Economic and military assistance to the Salvadoran government leapt from a mere $9.5 million in fiscal 1979 to $149 million in 1981. The fruit of this aid was a rural counterinsurgency campaign characterized by wholesale attacks on peasant villages thought to support the insurgency. Hundreds of thousands of refugees fled the country.

Once the 1980–81 urban terror had succeeded in eliminating most of the popular organization in the cities, elections were called for a constituent assembly in March 1982. This U.S.-inspired effort to improve the government's image resulted in a contest between the conservative wing of Duarte's Christian Democratic Party and several extreme-right parties; in the prevailing climate of terror, left politicians refused to participate. The Christian Democrats won slightly more than a third of the vote, while the extreme-right ARENA party won a quarter.

U.S. Counterinsurgency

The Salvadoran army and security forces grew from 13,250 men in 1980 to 53,000 in 1986, and acquired dozens of helicopters and a variety of ground-attack aircraft, including lethal AC-47 gunships. When the armed forces faltered in late 1983 and the guerrillas scored a string of high-profile military successes, Washington took a much more direct role in the day-to-day management of the war, reorganized the Salvadoran command structure, and, from a base in Honduras, began an intensive program of aerial reconnaissance of the Salvadoran countryside.

From the beginning, the counterinsurgency has been aimed largely at civilians, in an effort to break down the guerrillas' support structure. Initially with battalion-sized sweeps, more recently by means of aerial bombardments, the military has tried to force peasants to flee contested zones—a practice that *The New York Times* called "the cutting edge of the government's counterinsurgency strategy."[10]

U.S. economic and military aid totaled $437 million for fiscal 1986. Much of what is designated "economic" either has actually been military or has been used for "development" projects intimately linked with the counterinsurgency.[11] At the same time, Washington continued its efforts to fashion a credible facade of civilian rule. A presidential election in 1984, held under similar conditions to the election of 1982, produced a victory for Duarte. Some $10 million in U.S. funds was supplied to his campaign.[12]

Within the United States and on an international level, the Reagan administration worked to polish the military's tarnished human rights record by pressuring for a reduction of death-squad activities—efforts that Defense Minister Vides Casanova bluntly recognized as being "worth billions of aid for the country."[13] Political killings have fallen from the levels of the 1980–81 campaign of terror, although they have continued at a rate of several thousand a year. No Salvadoran officer has ever been tried and convicted for human rights violations.

What have been the results of six years of counterinsurgency in El Salvador, paid for by the United States? Militarily, this policy has only prolonged the war. Although massive amounts of U.S. aid and training have staved off an FMLN victory, the insurgents have adapted to changes in military strategy by the Salvadoran armed forces, conducting a war of attrition in all 14 provinces that continues to take a high toll in armed forces casualties.[14]

Fruits of War

Economically, the country is in shambles. In 1985 alone, damages to infrastructure and export crops totaled over $200 million.[15] Given the uncertain business climate, capital flight has been massive, and both domestic and foreign investment are stagnant. Not surprisingly, the war years have brought large budget deficits, an inflation rate of 30 percent in 1985, a 75 percent drop in export earnings from manufactured goods, and a rapid plunge in the standard of living of most Salvadorans. One-half of the annual budget is currently spent on defense.[16]

81

Five Countries, Five Realities

Although most Salvadorans are already in desperate straits, the Duarte administration implemented two packages of severe austerity measures in 1986 in order to pay for its war effort. Large quantities of U.S. aid, remittances from Salvadorans living abroad, and good coffee prices have also helped avoid bankruptcy.[17]

Politically, the military remains firmly in control of the government, and civilian politics is limited to a narrow segment from center-right to ultra-right. Duarte, despite campaign pledges, has been unwilling or unable to hold any serious talks with the FMLN, prosecute human rights violators, or enact meaningful agrarian reform, which is blocked by the constitution approved in 1983 by the rightist-controlled Constitutional Assembly. His remaining power is based largely on the fact that the military sees him as essential to getting the U.S. Congress to continue approving aid. The "centrist" government that Washington sought to foster has not taken root.[18]

Duarte's isolation has increased as unions and peasant organizations have expressed growing discontent at the same time as business and right-wing sectors have intensified their opposition.[19] The number of strikes has risen sharply. In February 1986, the National Salvadoran Workers' Union (UNTS), the largest and most pluralistic labor alliance in the history of El Salvador, was formed by several groups including peasant and worker organizations that once supported the Duarte government. UNTS has called for economic and social reform, democratic freedoms, peace through a process of dialogue and negotiation, self-determination, and national sovereignty.[20]

El Salvador's problems were compounded by the earthquake of 10 October 1986, which left over 1,200 dead and 150,000 people homeless and caused close to $1 billion in damage.[21] The government's poor handling of relief efforts has further eroded Duarte's political base.

Prospects for Reconciliation

Popular sentiment in El Salvador insists upon both reform and peace. There has arisen in recent years a broadly based opposition that strongly supports dialogue with the FMLN. Polls taken before the 1984 elections revealed that 70 percent of all Salvadorans considered the war and the economy to be the country's principal problems, and that 51 percent favored dialogue as the best means of resolving these problems; only 10 percent advocated the policy of the Salvadoran military and the Reagan administration, which is to vanquish the insurgency by force of arms.[22] The Roman Catholic Church remains an important force in Salvadoran politics, speaking out forcefully against attacks on civilians, and has been a mediator in contacts between the FMLN and FDR and the Salvadoran government. Some Protestant denominations, such as the Lutherans, have also been very active in relief and aid, and have, on occasion, been targets of right-wing retaliation.

The demilitarization of Central America under Contadora auspices, accompanied by a cutoff of U.S. war-related aid, would greatly increase the pressure on the Salvadoran government to reach a negotiated solution. Negotiations will have to address a number of crucial issues, principal among which would be ensuring full political participation for all social forces, without fear of intimidation or assassination. This will require a thorough housecleaning of the army and security forces, and the dismantling of the death-squad apparatus.

A key transitional step would be a cease-fire. Although partial Christmas cease-fires have been negotiated in the past, the FMLN has accused the military of noncompliance, and the Salvadoran armed forces have frequently declared their opposition to any measure of this sort. Nonetheless, both sides already have shown interest in partial accords to "humanize" the war—such as agreements on handling of prisoners and respect for the provisions of the Geneva conventions—as steps toward more

83

far-reaching solutions.[23] In the end, however, the successful implementation of a permanent cease-fire and the reduction and integration of these two armies depends on the establishment of a political process that would allow the resolution of issues without resort to violence. Ultimately, Salvadorans will have to implement a program of reforms, including agrarian reform, if there is to be permanent peace.

Land reform remains the most important underlying issue in El Salvador. The ultra-right and the oligarchy are set against any land reform, while the Christian Democrats favor the establishment of some peasant cooperatives based on the still to be implemented 1980 AID-sponsored land reform law. The FDR and FMLN support the redistribution of the traditional export sector to the peasantry through a broad program of land reform based on cooperatives and state farms, and the production of basic grains for the domestic market.

Prospects for a New Policy

Instead of fueling the Salvadoran civil war, Washington should work to end it. The United States has heavily supported the efforts of the Salvadoran military to defeat revolution in that country, at the price of many thousands of lives and the further strengthening of the anti-democratic military. In the process, the Salvadoran government has become almost wholly dependent upon the United States. Washington's first step must be to stop bankrolling a policy of military victory for one side and to cut off aid for waging war. Further U.S. economic aid should be made dependent on the Salvadoran government's progress in achieving a cease-fire and a negotiated settlement and on its compliance with internationally recognized human rights standards.

A new policy must recognize the profound importance of the mobilization that has taken place in El Salvador over the last decade and a half, and understand that any arrangement that excludes the country's majority from political power will fail.

Under conditions of a workable negotiated settlement, the United States can and should contribute toward reconstruction and development in El Salvador. Without such a settlement, U.S. aid will continue to be wasted. Development without reform— war or no war—is a contradiction in terms.

The United States also needs to adopt a more enlightened policy toward the hundreds of thousands of Salvadoran political refugees in the United States. Political asylum and "extended voluntary departure" status should be granted to these refugees, and community-level assistance for them should be encouraged. Already in existence in the United States is a network of private groups and church and community organizations dedicated to helping refugees from El Salvador and elsewhere in Central America. This "sanctuary movement" aims to shelter refugees who fear being sent home. The work of these organizations suggests that people-to-people contact can become an important part of a new policy toward El Salvador.

Notes

[1] Source for number of deaths in the Salvadoran civil war is *Washington Post*, 4 June 1986. Estimates of Salvadoran refugees living in Mexico, Honduras, Nicaragua, Costa Rica, and the United States range from 600,000 to 750,000 (see United Nations Human Rights Commission, *Report on UNHCR Assistance Activities in 1984–1985*, 5 August, 1985), while the number of displaced persons living in camps inside El Salvador was estimated to be between 525,000 and 700,000 in late 1985 (see United States Agency for International Development, "El Salvador Displaced Persons Program," Internal memorandum, San Salvador, 14 November 1985; and also Washington Office on Latin America, "Common Questions on El Salvador: The War and Human Rights," Winter 1986). Figure for war damages from World Bank estimate cited by *Washington Post*, 12 December 1983.

[2] *Latinamerica Press*, 22 May 1986.

[3] Thomas, Anderson, *Matanza* (Lincoln, Neb.: University of Nebraska Press, 1971).

[4] Robert Williams, *Export Agriculture and the Crisis in Central America* (Chapel Hill, N.C.: University of North Carolina Press, 1986).

[5] Laurence Simon and James Stephens, *El Salvador Land Reform 1980–1981: Impact Audit* (Boston: Oxfam America, 1981).

[6] The exception was the U.S.-fostered Unión Comunal Salvadoreño, created in the 1960s as part of the Alliance for Progress.

[7] Stephen Webre, *José Napoleón Duarte and the Christian Democratic Party in Salvadoran Politics: 1960–1974* (Baton Rouge, La.: Louisiana State Press, 1979).

[8] *Boletín Internacional del Socorro Jurídico del Arzobispado de San Salvador* 40 (15 May 1982): 3–6.

[9] Allan Nairn, "Behind the Death Squads," *The Progressive*, May 1984.

[10] James LeMoyne, "Bombings in El Salvador Appear to 'Bend the Rules'," *The New York Times*, 20 December 1985.

[11] Rep. Jim Leach, Rep. George Miller, and Sen. Mark O. Hatfield, *U.S. Aid to El Salvador: An Evaluation of the Past, A Proposal for the Future* (Arms Control and Foreign Policy Caucus, February 1985). See also the discussion in Richard Alan White, *The Morass* (New York: Harper & Row, 1984), 218–26.

[12] See Terry Lynn Karl, "After La Palma: The Prospects for Democratization in El Salvador," *World Policy Journal* 2 (Spring 1985): 313–17, on the U.S. role in sponsoring elections and AID funding of the UPD labor federation. For CIA financing of the elections see *Time*, 21 May 1984.

[13] Despite these efforts, a report of the U.S. Senate Select Committee on Intelligence found that "numerous Salvadoran military and security forces as well as other official organizations have been involved in encouraging or conducting death-squad activity or other violent abuses." See U.S. Congress, Senate Select Committee on Intelligence, *Recent Political Violence in El Salvador*, 5 October 1984; and James LeMoyne, "A Salvador Police Chief Vows an End to Abuses," *The New York Times*, 1 July 1984.

[14] The army reported that 2,834 soldiers were killed, wounded, or missing between 30 June 1984, and 30 June 1985—only slightly lower than the total of 3,108 for the previous 12 months. See *The New York Times*, 13 July 1985.

[15] James LeMoyne, "Salvadoran Rebels Have Learned to Dodge the Bullets," *The New York Times*, 5 January 1986.

[16] See *Latinamerica Press*, 22 May 1986. Also see Banco Central de Reserva, *Presupuesto Monetario de 1986* (San Salvador, El Salvador: 1986), cited in *El Salvador Boletín de Análisis e Información* 20, Centro de Investigación y Acción Social (January–February 1986): 2.

[17] Foreign financing now equals 53 percent of El Salvador's export earnings; without this constant influx of foreign funds, the fiscal deficit of $542 million would approximately double. The country's foreign debt of $2.5 billion grew 100 percent between 1978 and 1985. Most foreign funds come from AID; between 1978 and 1984, AID granted $1.87 billion to El Salvador. *Latinamerica Press*, 22 May 1986.

[18] See Kenneth Sharpe, "El Salvador Revisited: Why Duarte Is in Trouble," *World Policy Journal* 3 (Summer 1986): 473–93.

[19] James LeMoyne, "Duarte's Foes Call Strike in Effort to Oust Him," *The*

New York Times, 22 January 1987; and "After Parades and Promises, Duarte Flounders in Salvador," *The New York Times*, 16 February 1987.

[20] The first strike activity since the virulent repression against the labor movement of 1980 began in 1984. At least 37,000 workers took part in work stoppages in the Social Security Institute, the Salvadoran Teachers' Union, and various financial institutions and won a 10 percent public-sector wage increase. UNTS represents approximately 350,000 workers organized in cooperatives, unions, and associations, and includes some of the peasant and workers' associations established and controlled during the last 20 years by AID and/or AIFLD (American Institute for Free Labor Development).

[21] United Nations Economic Commission on Latin America and the Caribbean, *The 1986 San Salvador Earthquake: Repercussions and Assistance Required*, 16 December 1986. This report points out that the total damage represents about 25 percent of El Salvador's gross domestic product, and that by contrast, "though the total damage caused by the earthquake which struck Mexico City in September 1985 was four times higher, it represented barely 2 percent of the country's gross domestic product."

[22] These polls, obviously limited in their reliability because of the atmosphere of intimidation in which they were conducted, represent one of the few indicators of public opinion in El Salvador. The statistics favoring negotiations are particularly surprising in light of the fact that in early 1984 it was difficult to express support for negotiations—an FDR-FMLN position—without risking reprisals from the right. See Ignacio Martín-Baró and Victor Antonio Orellana, "La Necesidad de Votar: Actitudes del Pueblo Salvadoreño ante el Proceso Electoral de 1984," *Estudios Centroamericanos: Las Elecciones Presidenciales de 1984*, April–May 1984: 225–56.

[23] The commanders of both armies have made significant statements regarding their support for humanization and dialogue. The chief of staff of the Salvadoran Armed Forces, General Adolfo Blandón, stated that the war has "hurt 99 percent of the Salvadoran people, and we all want to end it" and that "we must consider ways of ending it, because we are not going to end it by bullets alone." "Evaluación de las operaciones Fenix y Carlos," *Proceso*, San Salvador, 17 February 1986. FMLN commander Joaquín Villalobos has frequently stated his support for humanization and dialogue. See, for example, "El estado actual de la guerra y sus perspectivas," *Estudios Centroamericanos*, March 1986.

9
Guatemala

Even by the bloodiest standards, Guatemala's last three decades have been characterized by extraordinary violence on the part of the armed forces, who in recent years have built a near-totalitarian system to regiment the lives of the rural population. Facing bankruptcy and international condemnation, the military in 1984 held elections for a Constituent Assembly, followed by an honest presidential ballot in 1985 that resulted in the election of Christian Democrat Vinicio Cerezo. But the new government has not only refused to investigate past human rights abuses, it has failed to prevent new ones. Guatemala has a military government with a civilian face, and fundamental reform seems as far away as ever.

History: Reform and Reaction

Guatemala's history has been shaped by the concentration of economic and political power in the hands of a small elite, backed by the army. Like El Salvador, it had a coffee, cotton, and sugar aristocracy; and like Honduras, it had the United Fruit Company, which owned large banana plantations and held vast tracts of land in reserve. But there are two important differences between Guatemala and those two nations.

In most of Central America, the original Indian populations were stripped of their cultural identity and took on the Hispanic (or *ladino*) culture and language of their conquerors. In

Guatemala, however, Indians still make up the majority of the population and have kept their language, culture, and identity. Most of them survive by a combination of subsistence farming and ill-paid seasonal work on coastal plantations.

The second difference is that in the late 1940s and early 1950s, Guatemala enjoyed a period of progressive democracy, comparable to that in Costa Rica in the 1940s. A reformist military revolt in 1944 was followed by elections and a remarkable series of reforms and social legislation. But the second president, Jacobo Arbenz, put forward an agrarian reform program that threatened the interests of the United Fruit Company, which owned 2 percent of the nation's land and kept most of it idle. The program, of the type that President John F. Kennedy's Alliance for Progress would champion less than a decade later, would have redistributed 234,000 of the company's 550,000 acres, paying the company exactly the value that it had declared on the land for its taxes to the Guatemalan government.[1]

United Fruit used its close ties to the Dwight Eisenhower administration to lobby successfully for an anti-Arbenz policy. In a sequence of events that bears a striking resemblance to Reagan administration policy toward Nicaragua, the White House described Arbenz's government as "communist" and "totalitarian" and gathered an army of right-wing Guatemalans in Honduras for an invasion.

The docking of a Czechoslovakian freighter carrying arms provided the final excuse for a U.S.-backed invasion that ousted Arbenz and installed Colonel Carlos Castillo Armas, flown in on the U.S. ambassador's plane. United Fruit's land was saved from expropriation, hundreds of peasant and labor leaders were rounded up and shot, and over the next 30 years successive military governments killed more than 100,000 Guatemalans.[2] Today, Guatemala's pattern of land ownership is one of the most unequal in the world. Two percent of the population owns 80 percent of the land, whereas 90 percent of farm families own plots too small for even subsistence-level agriculture.[3]

The new military rulers not only reversed the reforms of the 1944–54 period, they also became businessmen in their own right, and by the late 1970s they constituted a significant part of the economy. Generals amassed large estates and participated in business ventures, and corruption became institutionalized. Reformists in the army made one last try for power in an abortive coup in 1960, after which some progressive-minded officers left the military and started a guerrilla insurgency. They were largely defeated in the late 1960s with extensive counter-insurgency help from the United States.[4] During this period the army modernized and became the most militarily proficient, albeit brutal and corrupt, in Central America.

Guatemala's poor did not share in the economic development of the 1960s. A Guatemalan Indian has a life expectancy of only 45 years—fully 15 years less than his or her *ladino* counterpart.[5] Seventy-five percent of rural Guatemalans, or fully 45 percent of the entire population, are malnourished.[6] Because less than 25 percent of the population has access to safe water,[7] intestinal problems represent the leading cause of death among children under five.[8] The proportion of Guatemala's 1979 state budget devoted to education was about half that of El Salvador, Costa Rica, and even Somoza's Nicaragua.[9] The illiteracy rate remains the highest in Central America.

In this context a new wave of political organizing began in the mid-1970s, as the guerrilla organizations revived after the defeats of the 1960s. During 1977 and 1978 a broadly represen-tative and outspoken opposition movement sprang up, linking peasant associations, trade unions, church organizations, pro-fessional associations, and opposition parties. The government response was stepped-up repression, starting with the killing of key political leaders. Many of those who survived joined the insurgency.

The Role of the Church

Guatemala's Roman Catholic hierarchy encouraged the sort of anticommunism that contributed to the overthrow of the Arbenz government in 1954, but during the 1960s the Church began a slow but profound process of change. First through traditional pastoral work, later by participation in humanitarian and development programs, and finally through consciousness-raising among Indian and *ladino* peasants, the Church became a force for change and a threat to the regime. In the late 1970s and early 1980s, priests, nuns, and lay workers were ruthlessly persecuted, and more than a dozen (including a U.S. citizen) were murdered. Several dozen religious workers, including some Protestants, were forced to leave the country.

During the same period the military government backed a variety of Protestant fundamentalist sects in an effort to undermine Catholic allegiance among the population. This effort, supported by fundamentalist groups in the United States, reached a peak during the 1982–83 rule of General Efraín Ríos Montt, himself an evangelical Protestant. Currently the Roman Catholic Church is distanced from both the government and the insurgency but continues to work among the Indian and *ladino* poor.

A Scorched-Earth Policy

Acting on the famous dictum that a guerrilla is a fish swimming in the sea of the population, the Guatemalan army set out to drain the sea. In 1981 the army undertook a scorched-earth strategy that ultimately destroyed 400 Indian villages, many of whose inhabitants were systematically massacred.[10] Tens of thousands of Indian peasants were forced to flee, chiefly to Mexico. The counterinsurgency did not hit the insurgents themselves very hard, but it did kill or disperse much of their base of support.

The army then set out to restructure rural society, in a project of social engineering unprecedented in Latin America.[11] Strategic areas were named "poles of development," and local peasants were herded into camps under military supervision, heavily indoctrinated, and put to work on road-building projects that would permit the army easier access to remote areas. Throughout the peasant highlands, the population is controlled through restrictions on movement and the requirement that all able-bodied men participate in "civilian patrols," or antiguerrilla activity. An extensive network of informers has been established.

The purpose of the poles of development is to break up the traditional economy and to create a regimented and docile population that will not be inclined to support an insurgency. The insurgents, largely deprived of contact with the population, have been set back but continue to fight in isolated areas of the country.

Economic Troubles

Until the late 1970s, Guatemala seemed to be a successful example of economic growth without reform, at least for the small elite that ran its economy. Successive military-controlled governments pursued orthodox economic development policies designed to stimulate the export sector, minimize the role of the state, and keep the Guatemalan currency on a par with the U.S. dollar. Public debt was minimal; private investment, with few restrictions on foreign capital, provided virtually all development capital.[12] Growth during this period exceeded that of all other Central American nations except Costa Rica.

But the bloody counterinsurgency war of 1981–84 not only left the country with an extremely tarnished international reputation, it also exacted a heavy political and economic cost. U.S. military aid ceased in 1977 as a result of President Jimmy Carter's human rights policy, and the Reagan administration, although anxious to improve relations with the Guatemalan military, was blocked by Congress when it attempted to resume aid.[13]

By the early 1980s, the economic success story had ended. In 1982–83, Guatemala's gross domestic product dropped sharply and government deficits ballooned from a manageable 1 percent of GDP in the 1970s to well over 4 percent. By 1984 the government was spending twice as much as it took in,[14] and in 1985, payments on foreign debt took 40 percent of the country's export earnings.[15] Unemployment and underemployment rose from 31 percent in 1980 to 43 percent in 1984, inflation rose from 10 percent in the 1970s to over 50 percent in 1985, and real incomes fell across the board.[16]

The military's profligate spending on public works projects and on the counterinsurgency and the oligarchy's successful efforts to block tax increases[17] were primarily responsible for a situation of near-bankruptcy in 1985. The military clearly hoped that the election of a civilian president would bolster Guatemala's image abroad and open the flood gates of foreign aid and loans.[18]

Cerezo

A national assembly was elected in 1984 to write a new constitution, and in late 1985 presidential elections were held. The winner was Christian Democrat Vinicio Cerezo, whose party had suffered the murders of dozens of its activists in previous years. The Christian Democrats also gained a dominant position in the National Assembly.

Although he enjoyed widespread popular support at the outset of his term, Cerezo has not tried to go beyond the limits set on his power by the military; indeed, he has cemented relations with the armed forces and the oligarchy.[19] Before leaving office the armed forces enacted a series of laws by decree, including a blanket amnesty for themselves, and received Cerezo's pledge that there would be no land, commercial, or banking reforms, and no investigation of human rights abuses or prosecution of those responsible for such abuses. The military remains free of civilian control and has the power to name the Defense Minister; moreover, civilians have no say in the defense budget.[20] Cerezo has made some progress in replacing military officers with civilians in key government positions, although the police and other security forces remain firmly under military control.

In regional affairs, Cerezo's policy of active neutrality in regional conflicts is the same as that of the previous government of General Mejía Victores, although pressures from the military may at some point dictate a more pro-U.S. line.[21] He arranged the May 1986 summit meeting in Esquipulas in which the five Central American presidents affirmed their commitment to the Contadora peace process and the Central American Parliament, and agreed in principle to Central American integration.[22] Cerezo's government has refused to join the Tegucigalpa group (Honduras, El Salvador, and Costa Rica) in supporting U.S. efforts to isolate Nicaragua.

Human Rights

In recent years Guatemala has been the only Central American country in which no human rights group could even operate, so violent were the security forces and allied death-squads. Responsible for upwards of 50,000 killings in the 1980s alone, the military is perhaps the most brutal in Latin America.[23]

Since the elected civilian government has no power over the military, it is in no position to investigate past human rights abuses or to prevent new ones. Officers involved in gross violations of human rights remain at their posts.[24] Killings by the security forces continue to run at a level of at least 30–40 per month.[25] Cerezo fulfilled a campaign promise to disband the National Police's Department of Technical Investigations (DIT), whose agents were among the most notorious human rights abusers in the national security apparatus. But only one of the DIT agents was arrested; 100 were fired and 500 were offered positions in the equally repressive Special Operations Brigade. Not one of the DIT's leaders was among the 100 fired.[26]

Cerezo's chief domestic critic has been an organization called the Mutual Support Group (Grupo de Apoyo Mutuo, or GAM). GAM was formed in 1984 by family members of the "disappeared"—people kidnapped by the security forces and never seen again. Their purpose was to help members find missing relatives. But in March 1985, General Mejía Victores said publicly that "to seek the reappearance alive of those disappeared is a subversive act, and measures will be taken to deal with it." Leading members received death threats, then two of its officers were killed, one along with her young brother and infant son.

Cerezo himself accused the GAM of harboring subversive intentions. This accusation is a measure of how volatile the issue of the "disappeared" is, for it strikes at the heart of the legitimacy of the military's past and present power.

Cerezo also faces increased agitation from peasant organizations for some kind of agrarian reform. But this key issue also remains out-of-bounds for the civilian politicians. The economic elite still rejects even the most modest reform as an unacceptable precedent for further redistribution of land.

Prospects for a New Policy

The first thing that a new U.S. policy must recognize is that while Guatemala has civilian politics, it does not enjoy democracy. The Cerezo government should not be written off completely, but until conditions change the country must still be regarded as a military dictatorship. Unfortunately, Reagan administration policy has placed more value on the appearance of democracy than the substance, as the hollow "democratizations" of El Salvador and Honduras illustrate.

The principal aim of a new U.S. policy must thus be to

encourage a truly democratic transition in Guatemala. A new policy must condition any aid on firm standards of human rights practice, as well as political and labor rights. Every effort should be made to work with elected civilian officials, who must play a crucial role if Guatemala is to make a peaceful transition; but until then, all military assistance should be denied.

A transition to democracy implies tackling the human rights taboo, first by ending abuses and accounting for the "disappeared." Land reform will also be necessary to achieve peace in Guatemala.

A new policy should put the United States on the side of the country's majority, supporting efforts by urban workers and peasants, Indian and *ladino*, to organize and press for participatory democracy. Once a transition has been accomplished, U.S. economic aid should be directed to programs that help the poor majority and contribute toward fulfilling basic needs.

A new policy, finally, should emphasize contact between Guatemalans and U.S. citizens, both as an aspect of development programs and in order to cement better relations. The best place to start is at home: Guatemalan refugees in the United States should not be forced to return home against their will, but allowed to stay until government-sponsored violence ends.

Notes

[1] A third, somewhat more subtle difference is the greater strength of the Guatemalan state, and its links to business activities and the civilian elite. With a better rural and manufacturing infrastructure than its Central American neighbors, Guatemala has thus been able to build a strong army without heavy reliance on the United States. For general surveys of Guatemalan politics, see Robert Trudeau and Lars Schoultz, "Guatemala," in Morris J. Blachman, William M. LeoGrande, and Kenneth Sharpe, eds., *Confronting Revolution* (New York: Pantheon, 1986); Susanne Jonas, "Guatemala: Land of Eternal Struggle," in Ronald Chilcote and Joel Edelstein, eds., *Latin America: the Struggle with Dependency and Beyond* (New York: Schenkman, 1974); and George Black, Milton Jamail, and Norma Chinchilla, *Garrison Guatemala* (New York: Monthly Review Press, 1984).

[2] For estimates of the number of deaths, see Thomas P. Anderson, *Politics*

in Central America (New York; Praeger, 1982), 23; Stephen Schlesinger and Stephen Kinzer, *Bitter Fruit: The Untold Story of the American Coup in Guatemala* (Garden City, N.Y.: Doubleday, 1982), 247; George Black, "Under the Gun," in NACLA, *Report on the Americas* 19 (6): 11; George Black, "Introduction," in Mario Payeras, *Days of the Jungle* (New York: Monthly Review, 1983), 5; Guatemalan Church in Exile, *Development: The New Face of War* 6 (April 1986): 21; El Salvador and Guatemala Committees for Human Rights/War on Want Campaign, *Out of the Ashes: The Lives and Hopes of Refugees From El Salvador and Guatemala* (London, 1985); *Central America Report* 12 (22 February 1985): 52.

[3] World Bank, *Guatemala: Economic and Social Position and Prospects* (Washington, D.C.: World Bank, 1979), 72.

[4] Walter LaFeber, *Inevitable Revolutions* (New York: W. W. Norton, 1983), 168–72.

[5] World Bank, op. cit., 9.

[6] *The New York Times*, 20 July 1982.

[7] World Bank, op cit., 23.

[8] Organization of American States Inter-American Commission on Human Rights, *Report on the Situation of Human Rights in the Republic of Guatemala* (Washington, D.C.: General Secretariat of the Organization of American States, 1981), 131.

[9] Ibid., 131.

[10] Guatemalan Church in Exile, *Development: The New Face of War* 6 (April 1986): 21; George Black, "Under The Gun," op. cit.: 16.

[11] See George Black, op. cit.

[12] World Bank, op. cit., 58, 82–83.

[13] But military sales continued. See Allan Nairn, "The Guatemalan Connection," *The Progressive*, May 1986: 20–22.

[14] Inforpress Centroamericana, *Guatemala: 1985 Election* (Inforpress, 1985), 15–18.

[15] Economist Intelligence Unit, *Quarterly Economic Review of Guatemala, El Salvador, Honduras* 3 (1986): 15.

[16] Inforpress Centroamericana, op. cit.: 18–19.

[17] Inforpress Centroamericana (op. cit.: 15) notes: "Tax income as a percent of GDP is one of the lowest in the world, coming in at 5.3 percent in 1984 (while in the rest of Central America it ranged from 12 percent to 31 percent). ... Indirect taxes are disproportionately high. ... Direct tax on income and wealth, be it personal or corporate, comprises less than a fifth of tax revenue in Guatemala, whereas in other countries with a market economy it is generally closer to 80 percent."

[18] For the view that elections were part of the military's planning since 1982, see George Black, "Under the Gun," op. cit.: 22–23.

[19] For a discussion of the political situation, see Norma Stolz Chinchilla, "Guatemala: What Difference Does a Civilian Make?" *CENSA's Strategic Report*, December 1986.

[20] George Black, op. cit.: 23; *Central American Bulletin* 5 (February 1986): 3.

[21] American Friends Service Committee, *Neutrality in the Foreign Policy of Costa Rica and Guatemala: The Possibilities and Limits* (Philadelphia: AFSC, December 1986), 12–13.

[22] Instituto Histórico Centroamericano, *Envío* 5 (June 1986): 4–6; and *Honduras Update* 4 (June/July 1986): 6.

[23] Chris Krueger and Kjell Enge, *Security and Development Conditions in the Guatemalan Highlands* (Washington, D.C.: Washington Office on Latin America, August 1985).

[24] Allan Nairn and Jean-Marie Simon, "Bureaucracy of Death," *The New Republic*, 30 June 1986: 15.

[25] See the discussion in Americas Watch and British Parliamentary Human Rights Group, *Human Rights in Guatemala During President Cerezo's First Year* (February 1987), 29–38.

[26] Guatemalan Human Rights Commission, *Report to the Central American Commission on Human Rights* (Mexico: GHRC, 1986); Americas Watch Committee, *Guatemala: News In Brief* 1 (February–April 1986): 5; *Central America Bulletin* 5 (May 1986): 4; and Nairn and Simon, op. cit., 14.

10

Honduras

Honduras stands out from its neighbors in three respects: the relative absence (until the mid-1980s) of repression, a weak national government, and the extreme poverty of most of its citizens (average income and life expectancy are the lowest in the region). A history of domination by U.S. banana companies has left Honduras with a small military and civilian elite accustomed to bargaining away the country's national sovereignty.

For this reason, and because of the geographical fact that Honduras shares long borders with El Salvador and Nicaragua, the Reagan administration chose Honduras for its base of military operations in the region. U.S. policy toward the country continues to be a function of policy toward Nicaragua and El Salvador; it has little to do with the needs and problems of Honduras. Honduras now finds itself host to some 6,000–10,000 contras, who, failing to seize any Nicaraguan territory, have instead occupied hundreds of square miles of Honduras. The contras have brought in their families, expelled some 8,000 Hondurans, and in some cases renamed Honduran towns (there is a "Little Managua" in a border region called "New Nicaragua").[1]

A permanent force of over 1,000 U.S. military personnel, along with numerous CIA operatives, maintains a network of bases for provisioning the contras, conducting reconnaissance of El Salvador and Nicaragua, and training U.S. troops.

History: Enclave Development

Swindled by English and French railroad developers in the 1850s and 1860s, and exploited by U.S. mining concerns in the 1870s, the Honduran elite has always been too fractionalized and weak to strike good bargains with foreigners. Thus, the country's economic development has never been geared to local needs.[2]

During the first 50 years of this century, the United Fruit Company and other U.S.-based concerns established vast banana plantations in the northern part of Honduras. These companies built their own port facilities and railroads, constructed towns for their workers, and organized the Honduran government to suit their own purposes. The result was "enclave development," which contributed little to Honduras's economy beyond the meager wages paid to the workers (many of them Caribbean blacks) who tended, picked, and carried the bananas.[3]

The banana plantations became the crucible of a powerful trade union movement. A series of militant strikes from 1916 to 1934 provoked repression from the Honduran military and company strike breakers, and during the dictatorship of General Tiburcio Carias (1933–48), the unions were all but destroyed. But in 1954, in a famous two-month strike against the United and Standard Fruit companies, Honduran workers won the right to unionize.[4]

Since the early 1960s, the U.S. government has tried to influence the Honduran trade union movement through the American Institute for Free Labor Development (AIFLD). A relatively privileged sector of Honduran trade unionism, under AIFLD's influence, has concentrated on limited demands while eschewing—and at times, sabotaging—broader popular efforts to improve the lot of the poor in Honduran society. The Honduran government has also periodically tried to co-opt and divide the labor movement. Nonetheless, unions and peasant organizations

100

show strong potential to promote change and support a democratic process.[5]

Underdevelopment

Outside the banana enclaves, most of Honduras remained undeveloped. Until 1969 the country lacked an all-weather road linking the Atlantic and Pacific coasts. The lack of roads and railways, combined with mountainous topography and few navigable rivers, has been a powerful brake on Honduran development.

Yet Honduras's historic underdevelopment contained a paradox. Because bananas were grown in lowland areas previously uncultivated because of yellow fever, highland peasants were not pushed off their land by banana cultivation. The lack of major export production outside the foreign-owned enclaves meant that a powerful local oligarchy did not emerge. Rather, elites in the towns and thinly populated hinterlands either raised cattle for local markets or carried out minimal retail trade; until recent decades, their relations with the peasantry were more paternalistic than exploitative.[6] In El Salvador, Nicaragua, and Guatemala, coffee and cotton planters came into direct competition with peasants for land, and the military used violence to keep the poor in check. In Honduras the armed forces were relatively small, poorly trained, and more corrupt than repressive.

Pressure on the land intensified after World War II, when big landowners stepped up production of sugar, cattle, and timber for the world market. Honduras today has a highly unequal distribution of land: 60 percent of the country's agricultural land is divided among only 6 percent of its farms.[7] Fully one-third of the country's agricultural land, owned by big landowners, lies idle. Most Hondurans are subsistence farmers, and there are an estimated 200,000 landless farmworkers.[8]

This agrarian economy has not served Honduras well. The

country relies on agricultural and commodities exports for over 80 percent of its export earnings; in 1984, bananas and cotton together accounted for 53 percent of all exports.[9] Not only have prices for these commodities fallen in recent decades relative to the costs of imports, but much of Honduras's foreign exchange earnings have accrued to the foreign companies that dominate the nation's commercial and financial sectors.[10]

A further drain on capital has been service payments on Honduras's $2.6 billion foreign debt, which soaks up 40 percent of export income.[11] The country had meager capital resources to begin with, as foreign (mainly U.S.) companies have dominated the banking and commercial sectors and controlled much of the domestic market for consumer goods.[12]

These problems have been dramatically worsened by the economic policies dictated from Washington, which have forced Honduras to lift restrictions on foreign firms, reduce already-minimal social spending, and concentrate on export industry.[13] Moreover, by drawing Honduras into the contra war against Nicaragua, the United States has frightened investors, and the massive inflows of U.S. economic aid have been directed more to helping the country pay off its foreign creditors than to alleviating poverty. The primary beneficiaries have been the small group of army officers and businessmen involved in foreign trade. Unemployment is now at least 25 percent, staple foods must be imported, and there is little new investment.[14]

"Democratization" and Militarization

In 1980 the Jimmy Carter administration, alarmed by the success of the Sandinista revolution in Nicaragua, persuaded ruling General Policarpo Paz García to permit the election of a civilian government in exchange for increased U.S. military and economic aid. A Constituent Assembly was duly elected in April 1980, and presidential elections followed in November 1981. Before the 1981 elections the military forced the two traditional parties, the Liberals and Nationals, to agree that the armed forces would remain independent and exempt from investigation (mainly to prevent the exposure of massive corruption), would control foreign policy, and would have a veto over cabinet appointments. The Liberals won, and their standard-bearer, Roberto Suazo Córdova, was sworn in as president in January 1982. Suazo then named as head of the armed forces a young colonel, Gustavo Alvarez Martínez, a visceral anticommunist.[15] He and Suazo were prepared to work with Washington.[16]

In 1982 the Reagan administration was laying the groundwork for its attempt to overthrow the government of Nicaragua. Honduras would be used as a base, just as it had been for the 1954 overthrow of Jacobo Arbenz in Guatemala and the abortive 1961 Bay of Pigs attack on Cuba.[17]

In order to fit Honduras into U.S. plans, however, it was necessary to redesign its foreign policy. Honduras's traditional enemy is El Salvador, at whose hands the Honduran army suffered a humiliating defeat in the 1969 war. On the other hand, relations with postrevolutionary Nicaragua were reasonably good in 1979 and 1980.[18] Although conservative Hondurans found the Nicaraguan revolution alarming, Honduras had never had particularly good relations with Nicaraguan dictator Anastasio Somoza, and Honduran authorities did little to stop Sandinista militants from traveling through their country during Nicaragua's revolutionary war.

Under Alvarez, however, the Honduran military became deeply involved in the Reagan administration's effort to overthrow the Sandinistas. Early in 1982, U.S.-Honduran military exercises began in eastern Honduras, near the Nicaraguan border. Their main purposes were to construct camps and roads for the contras and to mask the supply of arms to those forces. Ever since, larger and larger "exercises" have been held in various parts of Honduras.[19]

The country's poor internal transportation network required the building of numerous roads and airstrips in order to supply contra camps spread out along the remote Nicaraguan frontier.

The main supply base, at Aguacate, comprises several warehouses, a hospital, and a paved 8,000-foot airstrip capable of accommodating large transport aircraft. Other facilities were built at Puerto Lempira and Mocorón in the Atlantic Coast region, and at Jamastrán and the Las Trojes area above north-central Nicaragua.

The Pentagon's secondary goal in Honduras was to assist the Salvadoran military in its own counterinsurgency. In 1980–81, Honduran troops cooperated with their Salvadoran counterparts in two well-publicized massacres of Salvadoran peasants trying to flee into Honduras.[20] Salvadoran soldiers and paramilitary personnel were permitted to enter refugee camps in Honduras to kidnap fellow-countrymen they suspected of subversive activities.[21] More than 20,000 Salvadorans remain in refugee camps in Honduras despite harassment by Honduran authorities and periodic efforts to move the camps away from border regions, so as to put them out of reach of more refugees.

In July 1983 the United States opened a training center at Puerto Castilla, on the Honduran Atlantic Coast, for Salvadoran troops. The Pentagon, forbidden to send more than 55 advisers to El Salvador, and lacking the resources to fly thousands of Salvadoran troops to the United States for instruction, saw Honduras as a cheap alternative.[22] This was widely resented by Hondurans, as their border dispute with El Salvador remains unresolved.

In 1984, U.S. aircraft, equipped with sophisticated infrared sensors, began patrolling the skies of El Salvador from the Palmerola base, headquarters of the U.S. military presence. The United States also maintains a variety of radar and monitoring facilities in Honduras for carrying out surveillance of Nicaragua and for supplying the contras with intelligence.

The Honduran armed forces grew from 14,000 troops in 1979 to 23,000 in 1984, as it acquired new artillery, helicopters, and equipment and training of all kinds. U.S. military aid increased from $4 million in fiscal 1979 to $78 million in 1983. But most alarming was the unleashing, under Alvarez, of a repressive campaign against trade union, church, student, and opposition leaders. With the financial backing of wealthy right-wing businessmen, Alvarez established a clandestine network of prisons into which over a hundred Hondurans disappeared.[23] In 1982–83, over 150 people were assassinated, and hundreds more were tortured, imprisoned, or forced into exile.[24] Repression on this scale, and the sinister phenomenon of "disappearances," had been unknown in Honduras before 1981.

In early 1984, rising protest, impelled by the kidnapping of two prominent trade union leaders, was a key factor leading to Alvarez's ouster by junior officers. Alvarez had also sought to override the Supreme Council of the Armed Forces (COSUFA), a body of 20–30 senior officers that constitutes the de facto government of Honduras. COSUFA feared that Alvarez would lead Honduras into a war with Nicaragua, so enthusiastic was his backing for the contras.[25]

Since Alvarez's departure, human rights violations have declined but not ceased, and the repressive apparatus has remained largely intact.[26] However, the Honduran military has adopted a slightly tougher negotiating stance toward Washington and closed the Puerto Castilla training base for Salvadorans.

Honduras has maintained an embarrassed silence about the contras. The government usually officially denies the presence of contras, although it has also publicly refused to allow U.S. Green Berets to train the contras in Honduras. Wishing to avoid hostilities with Nicaragua, Tegucigalpa reached an understanding with Managua that, if warned in advance of Nicaraguan incursions against contra installations, it would pull its own troops out of those regions.[27] But Washington has put considerable pressure on Tegucigalpa to adopt a more aggressive stance toward Nicaragua, forcing the Honduran government to request emergency military aid in March 1986, after Nicaraguan troops pursued contras across the border. In December 1986, apparently in response to further U.S. pressure and following a border engagement that resulted in the death of a Honduran soldier, Honduran aircraft bombed the Nicaraguan town of Wiwilí.

The contras have generated widespread opposition among Hondurans who were forced to flee from the border areas as the contras consolidated their hold over those regions. The Honduran Association of Coffee Producers is seeking $50 million in damages from the United States for the contras' depredations.

The Roman Catholic Church has deplored the increases in prostitution, venereal disease, and crime around U.S. bases. A variety of union, peasant, and professional associations have also come out against the U.S. and contra military presence.

The problems created by the U.S. military presence are another indication of the vast difference between Honduras's needs and the aims of U.S. policy. Honduran academic Victor Meza said in 1984 that "Honduras is little more to the United States than a geographic space . . . a staging area . . . from which it exercises its military and political power to contain the Sandinista revolution and to strike at the Salvadoran insurgents. But Honduras is more than that. It is a country with its own problems and difficulties."[28]

Democratization

Since Honduras lacks the decades-old patterns of wholesale political repression that afflict Guatemala and El Salvador, prospects for peaceful democratization in conditions of de-militarization are relatively good.[29] But Honduran politics has long been run on the basis of favoritism, patronage, and corruption, rather than popular participation.[30] And with the Honduran military and the United States holding the balance of power in the country, civilian politics remains a marginal arena contested by the squabbling factions of the two traditional parties.

In recent years a diverse opposition movement has developed

and begun to debate issues facing Honduras from a nationalist viewpoint. Peasant and labor organizations, along with student, church, and human rights groups, have taken an ever-more critical stand on domestic and foreign policies.

The Roman Catholic Church is relatively weak institutionally, and it lacks native clergy. At the national level, the Church is timid in denouncing human rights violations and unwilling to enter into direct confrontations with military or government authorities. But priests and bishops in the south braved repression during the 1960s and 1970s to support peasant demands for agrarian reform, and the Church could encourage a critical consciousness in Honduran society in the future. Protestants, particularly Mennonites, have worked with Salvadoran refugees and expressed opposition to militarization.

True democracy in Honduras would intensify pressures for redistribution of land. The country's poverty and the low prices its goods fetch on the world market limit the options, but agrarian reform, with genuine popular involvement, offers hope for raising the living standards of most Hondurans.

Prospects for a New Policy

The immediate aims of U.S. policy toward Honduras should be to reverse the unhealthy process of militarization imposed on that country since 1981 and, under the auspices of a Contadora treaty, to end the contra war. The United States should be prepared to accept those contras unwilling to take advantage of the Nicaraguan amnesty. Efforts to strengthen the armed forces must cease.

Washington should also encourage a peaceful resolution of the border conflict between El Salvador and Honduras, over which a war was fought in 1969. By arming both countries, the United States has inadvertently fueled an arms race between them and heightened the possibility of armed conflict in the future.

107

Five Countries, Five Realities

U.S. development assistance for Honduras should encourage agrarian reform and other measures directed at improving the lives of the poor. Honduras will continue to need assistance with capital investment for transportation and basic infrastructure projects.

The United States bears a paradoxical responsibility toward Honduras. Having dragged Honduras into a war that it wants no part of, Washington must resolve its own conflict with Nicaragua, end the cross-border fighting, and help Honduras recover from the impact of militarization. But Washington must also learn something even more difficult: to treat Honduras with respect as a sovereign nation, resisting the temptation to interfere in the affairs of this small country.

Notes

[1] Sam Dillon, " 'New Nicaragua' Takes Root in Honduras," *Miami Herald*, 11 June 1986. Dillon gives a figure of 2,000 square miles and adds that the contras have brought some 50,000 relatives with them. "Coffee Growers Denounce Contra Presence," *Tiempo*, 28 February 1986, translated in *Latin America Report*, Foreign Broadcast Information Service, FBIS, 10 June 1986: 78, gives a figure of 14,000 square kilometers. "Government to Decide on Contras for 'Security'," Agence France-Presse broadcast transcribed and translated in the *Latin America Report*, FBIS, 9 October 1986: 8. "Contras Allegedly Force Thousands to Flee Homes," *La Tribuna*, 16 May 1986, in *Latin America Report*, FBIS, 6 August 1986: 61. "Rendón, Montoya Challenge López on Contra Issue," *Tiempo*, 11 July 1986, in *Latin America Report*, FBIS, 22 September 1986: 57–58. "Impact of Contra Presence Assessed," *Tiempo*, 14 July 1986, in *Latin America Report*, FBIS, 25 September 1986: 55–56.

[2] Víctor Meza and Hector López Alvarenga, "La inversión extranjera en Honduras," *Boletín del Instituto de Investigaciones Económicas y Sociales* 22 (October 1973): 135–65.

[3] The workers were often paid in scrip or coupons good only at company stores. See Vilma Laínez and Víctor Meza, "El Enclave Bananero en la historia de Honduras," *Anuario de estudios centroamericanos* 1 (1974): 217.

[4] Richard Swedberg, *The Honduran Trade Union Movement 1920–1982* (Cambridge, Mass.: CAMINO, 1983).

[5] A. Douglas Kincaid, "We Are the Agrarian Reform: Rural Politics and Agrarian Reform," in *Honduras: Portrait of a Captive Nation*, Nancy Peckenham and Annie Street, eds. (New York: Praeger Press, 1986), 135–47.

[6] Jefferson Boyer, "From Peasant *Economía* to Capitalist Social Relations

Honduras

in Southern Honduras," *South Eastern Latin Americanist* 27 (March 1984): 1–22.
  ⁷ James W. Wilkie and Adam Perkal, eds., *Statistical Abstract of Latin America*, vol. 24, (Los Angeles: UCLA Latin American Center Publications, 1985): 37.
  ⁸ Economist Intelligence Unit, *Quarterly Economic Review of Guatemala, El Salvador, Honduras*, 1985 Supplement, 28.
  ⁹ From official Honduran government figures, as quoted in *La Tribuna*, 27 January 1986, translated in *Latin America Report*, FBIS, 20 March 1986: 69.
  ¹⁰ It is estimated that $15.7 million is repatriated from Honduras each year. See María Luisa Castellanos, "Honduran Economy: Fruits of Foreign Dependence," in *Latinamerica Press*, November 1985: 6. Capital flight between 1979 and 1984 is estimated at $800 million; see *Mesoamérica* 5 (May 1986): 4.
  ¹¹ Calculated from Comisión Económica para América Latina y el Caribe, *Notas para el estudio económico de América Latina y el Caribe, 1985—Honduras* (Mexico City: CEPAL, 1986): 44, 47.
  ¹² See Víctor Meza and Hector López Alvarenga, op. cit.: 135–65; and Rafael Del Cid, "Honduras: Industrialización, Empleo y Explotación de la Fuerza de Trabajo," *Economía Política* 13 (November 1976–June 1977): 51–129.
  ¹³ See John Cavanagh and Walden Bello, "Honduras Gets Marching Orders," *Counterspy* 6, no. 4 (July–August 1982): 39–40. See also more recent comments by Honduran presidential delegate Jaime Rosenthal on the Voz de Honduras network, 25 September 1986, as reproduced in the *Latin America Report*, FBIS, 26 September 1986: 3.
  ¹⁴ A recent World Bank report, quoted in *Tiempo*, puts unemployment at 25 percent. The head of the Association of Honduras Economists stated at the association's yearly convention in October 1986 that only 1.3 million of the 2.2 million Hondurans capable of working are employed—an unemployment rate of 41 percent. See Cadena Audio Video, 15 October 1986, translated in the *Latin America Report*, FBIS, 28 October 1986. On food imports, see "Corn Imports Increase," *La Tribuna*, 8 March 1986, translated in *Latin America Report*, FBIS, 7 July 1986: 58, 59.
  ¹⁵ Gregorio Selser, "Alvarez, un coronel con una política exterior particular," *El Día*, 10 April 1982.
  ¹⁶ For overviews of U.S. Honduran policy, see Philip Shepherd, "The Tragic Course and Consequences of U.S. Policy in Honduras," *World Policy Journal* 1 (Fall 1984): 109–54; and Mark Rosenberg, "Honduran Scorecard," *Caribbean Review* 12 (Winter 1983): 12–13, 39–42.
  ¹⁷ Gregorio Selser, "El papel que jugó en 1954 contra Guatemala y su analogía con el que hoy cumple," *El Día*, 3 July 1983.
  ¹⁸ "Honduras Goes Its Own Way," *This Week Central America and Panama*, 24 September 1979: 293.
  ¹⁹ See Fred Hiatt, "Entrenching in Honduras," *Washington Post*, 10 February 1986; also Colin Danby, "Tightening the Screws," *Honduras*

Update 2 (April 1984): 3–4; Stephen Goose, "Into the Fray: Facts on the U.S. Military in Central America," *The Defense Monitor* 13 (1984); National Action/ Research on the Military Industrial Complex, *Invasion: A Guide to the U.S. Military Presence in Central America* (Philadelphia: NARMIC, 1985); and Edward King, *Report on Military and Political Situation in Central America* (Boston: Unitarian Universalist Service Committee, 1984).

[20] Philip Wheaton, *The Iron Triangle: The Honduran Connection* (Washington, D.C.: EPICA, 1981).

[21] "Honduran-Salvadoran Military Complicity in Refugee Incidents," *Central America Report* 8 (5 December 1981): 379.

[22] Raymond Bonner, "U.S. Said to Plan a Military Base in Honduras to Train Salvadorans," *The New York Times*, 10 April 1983.

[23] Juan Méndez, *Human Rights in Honduras: Signs of the "Argentine Method"* (New York: Americas Watch, December 1982). Ramón Custodio, *Aspectos Jurídicos del terrorismo y del antiterrorismo en Honduras* (Tegucigalpa: Centro de Documentación de Honduras, 1983).

[24] Figures from the Honduras Documentation Center, as reported by Steve Lewontin, "Human Rights: Still Waiting," *Honduras Update* 3 (October 1984): 2. See also Lucila Funes de Torres, *Los Derechos Humanos en Honduras* (Tegucigalpa: Centro de Documentación de Honduras, 1984).

[25] Gregorio Selser, "El Desalojo de Alvarez, motivado por hartazgo de sus camarades. Suazo no sabía nada," *El Día*, 8 April 1984). Also see Marcia McLean, "Suazo Knew Nothing," *Honduras Update* 2 (May 1984): 1–4.

[26] Steve Lewontin, "Human Rights: Still Waiting," *Honduras Update* 3 (October 1984): 1–3; Ramón Custodio, *La Situación de los Derechos Humanos en Honduras, Enero–Octubre 1986* (Tegucigalpa: Comité para la Defensa de los Derechos Humanos en Honduras, 1986); and *The Human Rights Situation in Honduras 1986* (Somerville, Mass.: Honduras Information Center, 1987). Custodio reports that in 1986 there were 37 killings attributed to security forces and another 83 murders under suspicious circumstances, as well as four "disappearances." Since Alvarez's ouster, there have been a total of 30 "disappearances."

[27] Julia Preston, "Government Cedes Border Strip To Nicaraguan-Rebel Fighting" and Edward Cody, "Determined Sandinista Army Chases Enemy Across Frontier," *Washington Post*, 11 November 1986.

[28] Víctor Meza, "Recent Developments in Honduran Foreign Policy and National Security," in Mark B. Rosenberg and Philip L. Shepherd, eds., *Honduras Confronts Its Future* (Boulder, Colo: L. Rienner Publishers, 1986), 222.

[29] For further exploration of this question, see two articles by Philip Shepherd: "Honduras Confronts Its Future: Some Closing, but Hardly Final Thoughts," in Mark Rosenberg and Philip Shepherd, op. cit., and "Honduras," in Blachman, LeoGrande, and Sharpe, op. cit., 125–55.

[30] Ibid.

11

Costa Rica

For almost 40 years, Costa Rica has been the exception to the bloody Central American pattern of military coups, insurgency, and repression. Costa Rican exceptionalism has been built on the twin pillars of democratic reformism and a demilitarized society.

But recent years have brought a severe economic crisis, during which rural poverty and landlessness have worsened. The remedies prescribed by the International Monetary Fund (IMF) have led to a weakening of the Costa Rican welfare state. In the long run, economic decline threatens the social contract that has given Costa Rica nearly four decades of reformist democracy and social peace.

Moreover, U.S. pressure on Costa Rica's government to take sides in the war against Nicaragua has significantly eroded the country's tradition of neutrality and spurred the buildup of its security forces.

An Exceptional History

Largely because it was spared the worst ravages of Spanish colonialism, Costa Rica entered the 20th century with a far less unequal distribution of land than that found in its neighbors to the north. Coffee producers did amass considerable wealth, acreage, and political clout, but their power was offset by a large class of independent small farmers. Throughout this century, except for two brief interludes (1917–19 and 1948–49), Costa Ricans enjoyed the benefits of civil liberties, an independent judiciary, and regular elections for a president and national assembly.[1]

Costa Rica's social welfare system was begun by reformist governments in the early 1940s. Backed by peasant and labor organizations, they put into place a progressive labor code, socialized health care, and social security. But the process was divisive, and it aroused opposition from the middle class and big landowners. When a conservative party apparently won the 1948 election only to have the result thrown out by the Congress, a civil war broke out. Opposition forces, led by Social Democrat José Figueres, took power in only six weeks.[2]

Perhaps Figueres's most important legacy during the year and a half that he ruled as part of a provisional junta was the abolition of the country's armed forces, a step incorporated into the Costa Rican constitution. Since then no Costa Rican government has been overthrown by or even seriously threatened with a coup, and the country has to this day a remarkably good human rights record compared to other countries in the region.

Figueres also kept most of the reformist legislation enacted during the previous eight years—and in some respects expanded it—but he also repressed trade unions that had agitated for the reforms, largely excluding them from the political process.[3] Repression of unions, particularly those representing banana workers, continues to this day.[4]

Through economic changes, Figueres sought to bolster the middle class against both the old coffee oligarchy and the lower classes, while maintaining and expanding a welfare system to prevent serious discontent among the poor. Figueres also used the expansion of the bureaucracy to create a constituency for his National Liberation Party among government workers.

Despite its abiding political myth as the land of the "yeoman farmer," Costa Rica's pattern of land ownership today does not differ markedly from that of the rest of Central America.[5]

112

Although an important class of small coffee-growers remains, the expansion of export agriculture in recent decades has had the same effect in Costa Rica as elsewhere—concentration of landholdings and elimination of smallholders and subsistence farming. A land reform program begun in 1961 has helped some peasant families, but there are many more peasant families in need than it can accommodate.[6] Peasant unrest and land invasions have increased markedly during 1986–7.

The Economic Crisis

Costa Rica's current economic crisis has both external and internal causes.[7] Externally, the 1970s brought an overall deterioration in the terms of trade: the country's agricultural exports brought in less at the same time as necessary imports, particularly oil, become more expensive. Rising interest rates in the 1980s hurt Costa Rica, which had borrowed heavily to finance its large public sector and trade deficit. By 1986 the country's foreign debt stood at $4 billion, producing one of the highest per capita debt burdens in the world. Half of Costa Rica's export earnings were used to service the debt in 1985; had it met all its debt commitments, the amount would have reached 70 percent.[8]

The recession of the early 1980s is by no means over. Growth in 1985 was only 0.9 percent—negative 1.7 percent on a per capita basis. In 1986, because coffee prices went up while oil prices and interest rates declined, growth was 3 percent—0.4 percent on a per capita basis.

The regional crisis has been a major factor in the decline in intraregional trade, which has been particularly damaging to Costa Rica. With a relatively strong industrial base, Costa Rica has prospered through trade within the Central American Common Market (CACM). But the regional conflict has interrupted intraregional trade flows.[9] CACM trade has fallen to half of what it was in 1980, and other Central American nations now owe Costa Rica $600 million.[10] Aside from a few foreign firms—mainly garment manufacturers that have been attracted by the incentives offered under the Reagan administration's Caribbean Basin Initiative—Costa Rica has attracted little foreign investment in recent years.

The country's debt and balance-of-payments deficits have made it increasingly vulnerable to financial pressures from the International Monetary Fund and political pressures from the United States. Both the State Department and the IMF have sought to dismantle the state sector and roll back social spending in such areas as food subsidies and subsidized credit to small farmers.[11] U.S. aid, originally promoted by congressional Democrats as a way to support democracy, has become a basic instrument for control in the Reagan administration's regional political-military strategy. U.S. leverage is substantial: aid to Costa Rica increased from $13 million in fiscal 1981 to $151 million in fiscal 1986.

Pressure to Militarize

In essence, the Reagan administration has agreed to keep the Costa Rican economy afloat in exchange for Costa Rican hostility toward Nicaragua.[12] As President Oscar Arias has said, "As long as there are nine *comandantes* in Nicaragua, we'll get $200 million a year from Washington in aid."[13]

Although most contra operations against Nicaragua have been carried out from Honduras, from the beginning U.S. strategists have viewed Costa Rica as a base and supply source for contras operating in southern Nicaragua. Washington has sought to carry out the same kind of airstrip and road construction in northern Costa Rica that it accomplished in Honduras in order to supply contra forces.[14] Costa Rica has on some occasions rejected U.S. construction plans. The current government, the object of a Nicaraguan World Court suit over contra activity, has tried to shut down contra facilities. Despite these efforts, however, Costa Rica has been dragged into a de facto alliance with Washington against Nicaragua.[15] Since 1982, Costa Rica has also played an increasing role in U.S. political and diplomatic efforts to isolate Nicaragua and frustrate the Contadora process.

Costa Rica's status as a demilitarized society has also been threatened.[16] The country still lacks a politically powerful institutional military. It is becoming harder and harder, however, to draw a clear distinction between the country's "security" forces and an army of the kind that is banned under the country's constitution. The security forces—the Rural and Civil guards—have more than doubled in size since 1979, to a total in 1987 of roughly 10,000 men under arms, with U.S. military training and weapons.[17] A civilian militia with another 10,000 members has also been formed. Since 1982, government spending on police and security forces has more than quadrupled.[18] Four counterinsurgency battalions have been trained since 1984, the first of which was created in complete secrecy by U.S., Israeli, and West German advisers.[19] U.S. advisers have been stationed at the Murciélago base near the Nicaraguan border.

In recent years a shadowy network of paramilitary groups has sprung up, with links to both the contras and the rightist paramilitary Movement for a Free Costa Rica (MCRL).[20] Numerous acts of violence in Costa Rica have been attributed to these groups and to various contra organizations. Costa Rica also harbors the region's biggest black market in arms, as well as a growing drug trade.

Another impact of the war has been a growing refugee population in Costa Rica. By the end of 1986 the country had absorbed at least 30,000 documented refugees, of whom over half were Nicaraguans.[21] But the more serious problem is that there are also 200,000 undocumented refugees, mostly Nicaraguans who arrived before 1979. Caring for the refugees has further strained the Costa Rican economy. The Nicaraguan community has also been fertile ground for contra recruiting, which Costa Rican authorities have had difficulty controlling.

The Roman Catholic Church, traditionally close to the progressive wing of the National Liberation Party, has backed the party's social welfare legislation and has spoken up for the country's poor. The Church, while continuing to support a policy of neutrality, has offered neither encouragement nor resistance to the country's involvement in the U.S. war against Nicaragua. San José is also the regional headquarters of several Protestant denominations. They have not, however, had much impact on national political life.

Prospects for a New Policy

Costa Rica will benefit greatly from a halt to the U.S. contra war against Nicaragua. A regional peace settlement under the auspices of Contadora offers Costa Rica the opportunity to regain its traditions of political neutrality. This would also make it easier to dismantle the fledgling paramilitary organizations within Costa Rica.

Regional peace and demilitarization could also help alleviate Costa Rica's economic crisis. Revitalized regional trade would stimulate the manufacturing sector. Given the attractiveness of Costa Rica's highly educated work force, peace would encourage the return of foreign investment.[22]

The case of Costa Rica demonstrates the need for a fundamental shift in U.S. economic policy. Current aid has not remedied Costa Rica's economic problems, both because it is part of a policy of war and because it addresses the symptoms while leaving the roots of the country's economic problems untouched. U.S. economic aid should be aimed at strengthening, rather than undermining, the country's social programs and mixed economy.

Costa Rica's tradition of peaceful civilian politics is precious. If the region can demilitarize, Costa Rica should be able to keep its reformist traditions.

Notes

[1] See the discussion in Morris Blachman and Ronald G. Hellman, "Costa Rica," in Morris J. Blachman, William M. LeoGrande, and Kenneth Sharpe, eds., *Confronting Revolution* (New York: Pantheon, 1986).

[2] Manuel Rojas, *Lucha social y guerra civil en Costa Rica* (San José: Editorial Porvenir, 1979); Walter LaFeber, *Inevitable Revolutions* (New York: W. W. Norton, 1983), 101–103; and Ralph Lee Woodward, *Central America: A Nation Divided*, 2nd ed. (New York: Oxford University Press, 1985), 225–28.

[3] Charles D. Ameringer, *Democracy in Costa Rica* (New York: Praeger, 1982).

[4] Philippe Bourgois, "Ethnic Diversity on a Corporate Plantation: The United Fruit Company in Bocas del Toro, Panama and Palamanca, Costa Rica" (unpublished Ph.D. dissertation, Stanford University, 1985), 402–404, ff. 1, 3, 424.

[5] John Weeks, "An Interpretation of the Central American Crisis," *Latin American Research Review* 21 (3): 41.

[6] F. Barahona Riera, *Reforma Agraria y Poder Político, el Caso de Costa Rica* (San José: Editorial Universitaria de Costa Rica, 1980), estimates that 18,078 rural households had benefited in 1975. But M. Seligson, "La Reforma Agraria en Costa Rica, 1942–1976: la Evolución de un Programa," *Estudios Sociales Centroamericanos* 7 (19): 15–82, estimates 11,306 beneficiary families in 1976. Both figures are quoted in Carmen Diana Deere, "Rural Women and State Policy: the Latin American Agrarian Experience," *World Development* 13 (9): 1037–53.

[7] See Richard Feinberg, "Costa Rica: The End of the Fiesta," in Richard S. Newfarmer, *From Gunboats to Diplomacy* (Baltimore: Johns Hopkins Press, 1984); Philip W. Rourk, *Equitable Growth: The Case of Costa Rica*, Case Studies in Development Assistance, No. 6 (Washington, D.C.: Agency for International Development, 1984); and Blachman and Hellman, op. cit. See also Marc Edelman, "Recent Literature on Costa Rica's Economic Crisis," *Latin American Research Review* 18 (2): 166–80.

[8] *Central America Report* 13 (9 May 1986): 129.

[9] See *Economic and Social Progress in Latin America, 1986* (Washington, D.C.: Inter-American Development Bank, 1986), 246.

[10] *Central America Report* 13 (11 April 1986): 97.

[11] Marc Edelman, "Back from the Brink," *NACLA Report on the Americas* 19 (November–December 1985): 37–48.

[12] Richard Meislin, "U.S. Said to Seek Costa Rica Shift," *The New York Times*, 11 May 1984; and *Neutrality in the Foreign Policy of Costa Rica and Guatemala: The Possibilities and Limits* (Philadelphia: American Friends Service Committee, 1987).

[13] Howard Banks, "Bankruptcy without Pain," *Forbes*, 29 April 1985: 110.

[14] "Contra y neutralidad: malabar imposible," *Pensamiento Propio* 4 (July

1986): 29–31. For an account of U.S. activity around the Santa Elena airstrip, see *The Tower Commission Report* (New York: Bantam Books, 1987), 470–75.

[15] Tim Coone, "Costa Rica Dismantles Nicaraguan Rebel Camp," *Financial Times*, 27 April 1985; Chris Hedges, "Costa Rica Shuts Down Contra Military Operations," *The Dallas Morning News*, 10 November 1986. See also Joel Brinkley, "Costa Ricans at Odds Over Question: Is U.S. Seeking to Militarize Nation?" *The New York Times*, 19 May 1985.

[16] Daniel Camacho, "'El antimilitarismo está profundamente arraigado,'" *Pensamiento Propio* 4 (November–December 1986): 8–10.

[17] Silvio Dobri, "Costa Rica About to Create an Army?" *Miami Herald*, 12 June 1983.

[18] *Central America Report* 13 (9 May 1986): 134.

[19] Ibid.

[20] "Overview of Clandestine Groups, Government Response," *Rumbo Centroamericano*, 25 April–1 May 1986, translated in *Latin America Report*, FBIS, 19 June 1986: 113–18.

[21] "Over 30,000 refugees in Costa Rica," *Uno más Uno*, 7 February 1987.

[22] Feinberg, op. cit., 107.

PART III
An Alternative U.S. Policy

Throughout the 1980s the United States has sought to dictate events in Central America, primarily through the use of allied or proxy military forces. The human and economic toll in the region has been outlined in Part I and detailed for each country in Part II. The economic, social, political, and moral costs to our own system are only now coming to public attention. The bankruptcy of current policy is clear. The urgent task is to construct and implement a sound alternative.

A policy of peace and development, founded on demilitarization and diplomacy, offers a more prudent and realistic course for the United States. The rationale for a fundamental policy change is clear: War and development are incompatible; war can only be ended through a prolonged process of diplomacy; and in the long run, development that does not combine social justice with growth will only destabilize. Inequitable development threatens peace in the future just as it has in the past.

12

New Realities, New Respect

Despite the current furor over Central America, there is substantial domestic agreement regarding the long-term objectives of the United States. We seek a region at peace, in which human rights are respected and democracy flourishes. We seek economic development that diminishes inequality and reduces deprivation and poverty, thus providing the basis for stability and sustained growth. We seek neighbors who resolve their disputes peacefully, through diplomacy and the rule of law. Finally, we seek policies that justify our role as a global power, demonstrating that a great nation can live peacefully and sensibly with a diversity of small neighbors.

If these are our goals, surely the present course is folly. Regional conflicts are presented as global conspiracies threatening our security. Initiatives for peace, law, and economic development are shelved until military victory against revolutionary forces can be achieved. With victory elusive, U.S. policy is reduced to using patchwork reforms as a cover for a slow escalation of violence. After almost seven years, billions of dollars, and thousands of lives, our long-term objectives are more remote than ever.

No balanced policy can be created unless we regain a sense of scale. The United States is the dominant economic, cultural, political, and military power in the region. The countries of Central America are small, most of their citizens are impoverished, and their material resources are not strategic. The five Central American republics have neither the political, military, nor economic strength to threaten the security of the United States. On the other hand, the United States inevitably has a significant influence on events in the region no matter what policies are pursued. Isolation is not only inadvisable; it is impossible. What is needed are judicious, measured, and constructive responses to developments that lie beyond the control but not the influence of the United States.

Once Central American dynamics are seen in clear perspective and proportion, the United States can respond with much greater confidence and benefit. As Parts I and II have shown, the old order is dying, the new is struggling to be born. This historic transition contradicts and defies the assumptions that have guided U.S. policy for over a century. Only by understanding these new realities can the United States fashion a viable alternative.

Popular Democracy

Throughout Central America, the failure of the old order has brought new actors onto history's stage. The Sandinista revolution, for example, brought together a remarkable mix of Marxists and Christians, of classes and interests. This pluralism is reflected, if not precisely duplicated, in contemporary popular mobilizations in El Salvador and Guatemala. Chapter 6 showed that grass-roots mobilization is vital to equitable economic development. The direct participation of peasants and workers, their challenge to the old order, is a component of the process through which a more equitable new order can be built.

For a long time the drama of Central American history has been directed by an oligarchic and military elite, supported by the United States. Now the region's majority is demanding a role in determining its own future. This new historical actor is a composite of peasants, agricultural and urban workers, migrants, and unemployed and underemployed people. It includes the indigenous populations, blacks and mulattos, most of the young (50 percent of the population is under 20), and women (traditionally exploited on the basis of gender as well as race and class). This immensely diverse population is increasingly finding voice and organizational expression in a continuing struggle for social, political, and economic participation.[1]

There is an intimate relationship between this popular mobilization and democracy in Central America. Typically in U.S. policy discussions, democracy is defined as and limited to elections and perhaps some improvement in human rights. A fuller and more authentic understanding of democracy is essential—an understanding that validates the rights of peasants, workers, and others not only to organize but also to make themselves heard and felt in the public arena—by marches, protests, and strikes if necessary.

In the past, U.S. policy-makers have viewed mass mobilization, protest movements, and the full richness of political participation in Central America as something to be avoided at almost any cost. In other words, while paying lip service to democracy, in practice the United States has sided with the dominant military and economic elites in openly discouraging or actively repressing democratic expressions of mobilization and protest—often characterizing such expressions as the provocations of "communists" or "radicals." It is for this reason that many Central Americans view U.S. policies as antidemocratic, despite Washington's protestations to the contrary.

Mobilization and protest, however, are not only inevitable in a demilitarized Central America, but actually essential to political life and equitable development. The power of entrenched elites to defend the deeply unjust status quo is so great that only vigorous grass-roots movements can stimulate and implement fundamental reforms. Either the United States must come to support real grass-roots democracy, or by default it will continue siding with elites in the name of "stability." This will call for a shift of historical vision quite alien to U.S. policies and pronouncements about democracy in the region.

Living with Nationalism

Given our own history of outspoken nationalism, first generated in the cauldron of the struggle for independence and the American Revolution, we are proud to remember Patrick Henry's "Give me liberty or give me death." Nevertheless, the United States has had significant difficulties in coming to terms with nationalism in the Third World. The Sandinistas' "*Patria libre o morir*" (a free homeland or death) is dismissed as rhetorical excess.

Yet the Sandinista slogan and others like it express a profound truth: For many Central Americans, their own dignity is inextricably linked to changed relationships with the rest of the world, and particularly with the United States. The existing century-old relationship—in which the United States has dominated local politics and economics, defined the acceptable limits to change, and intervened when it chose—is unacceptable to most Central Americans. Thus, Central American nationalism almost inevitably contains a large dose of what in the United States is perceived as anti-Americanism.

The United States, however, has no choice but to learn to live with Central American nationalism, for it will not go away. On the contrary, it is the most widely shared political perspective in the region, linking groups that are otherwise far apart on the political spectrum. A more mature U.S. policy would view this nationalism as essentially constructive. Not only does it provide a common meeting ground for otherwise contending groups, but it is the surest guarantee that foreign powers will not be welcome in Central America if they attempt to subordinate local interests to their own or impose alien strategies that do not respond to local needs.

The Contadora process, bringing together the major democracies of the hemisphere in an attempt to formulate conditions for a peaceful solution to the Central American crisis, provides dramatic testimony to the positive potential of nationalist sentiment in the region. A new, more realistic U.S. policy must not only accept these powerful currents of nationalism, but eventually embrace them as allies in the search for peace and development.

International Law

The Charters of the United Nations and the Organization of American States, along with almost all other contemporary international agreements, proclaim the sovereignty, territorial integrity, and equality of nations. Yet superpower behavior frequently tells a different story. From Afghanistan to Angola to Nicaragua, big powers violate the sovereignty and territorial integrity of smaller, weaker neighbors in blatant and often bloody disregard for their rights. In every corner of the globe, power politics constantly confronts principles of international law such as respect for sovereignty and self-determination.

Respect for the fundamental principles of international law must orient and discipline the exigencies of power politics in U.S. Central American policy. We cannot expect others to honor those principles if we so flagrantly violate them. Nor can we expect to regain minimal domestic consensus in the conduct of foreign policy until these values are acted on, not just hypocritically preached. At least in this instance, there is no need to abandon principles in the name of pragmatism; on the contrary, the most realistic course is also the most moral.

Adopting a principled policy of nonintervention and respect for sovereignty is thus the first step that Washington must take in order to bring peace to Central America. As argued in Part I, nonintervention in practice in Central America means demilitarization, and demilitarization in turn makes possible a frontal assault on the region's fundamental social and economic problems. But as we have also argued, development must be given a new meaning and take place in a different context. It is to these knotty problems that we now turn.

Note

[1] For further exploration of this topic see "Centro América 1979–85," *Envío* 5 (January–February 1986), and Orlando Núñez Soto, "Ideology and Revolutionary Politics in Transitional Societies," pp. 231–48 in Richard R. Fagen, Carmen Diana Deere, and José Luis Coraggio, eds., *Transition and Development: Problems of Third World Socialism* (New York: Monthly Review Press, 1986).

13
A Regional Alternative

A new U.S. policy toward Central America must embody a fundamental shift away from Washington's current approach to economic issues. At least six dramatic changes are required.*

1. *From bilateral to multilateral.* Current U.S. policy encourages maximal economic links between each individual country (except Nicaragua) and the United States. An alternative policy would encourage diversification of economic and political relations—with Europe, Canada, nonaligned nations of the developing world, and socialist countries—recognizing that by virtue of proximity and size the United States will always remain the key actor. Major partners in this multi-lateralism should be the larger Latin American nations to the south, whose economies are sufficiently diverse to offer many needed goods, services, and markets to Central America.

2. *From antiregional to regional.* Special economic incentives in the Reagan administration's Caribbean Basin Initiative actively discourage economic relations between Central American nations, giving preference instead to trade and investment from the United States. Just the opposite should be the case. A revitalized Central American Common Market is thus a high priority, as are closer relations with other countries in the greater Caribbean area.

---

* The discussion that follows focuses on United States economic relations with Central America, although all of the major points are relevant to relations with the Caribbean at large.

3. *From competitive to complementary.* Currently, Central American nations are pitted against one another in competition for external markets, attempting to export the same products and competing for private investment by offering cheaper labor and more favorable tax advantages. But Central American nations cannot grow individually at the expense of their neighbors. A new policy must encourage greater complementarity and cooperation between nations in production, commerce, and finance.

4. *From externally oriented to more-balanced growth.* Past growth in the region's economies has been driven by exports of a few primary commodities and light manufactures produced by cheap labor. Exports will always remain crucial to growth, but it is also necessary to strengthen internal and regional markets, process raw materials locally, and re-invigorate domestic output of staples and other foodstuffs.

5. *From opposition to diversity to respect for diversity.* Current U.S. policy favors those countries that embrace U.S. hegemony, military alliances, investment, and development strategies, while striving to punish and even destroy governments that follow more independent economic and political policies. A new policy would respect our neighbors as sovereign nations, even when they modify their political models or diversify their economic relationships. A Central America safe for diversity would also be a region in which democratic practices stood a better chance of becoming the norm rather than the exception.

6. *From short- to longer-term perspectives.* Current economic policies are short-sighted and short-term. They pressure Central Americans to produce and export more of the same traditional agro-products, diversifying a bit if private capital willing to invest in new ventures can be attracted to the region. Over the longer run, this strategy simply locks Central American nations into a pattern of crises and under-development. A viable alternative would help the region break out of this vicious circle. Fundamental reforms are

needed, so that Central America's future will not be mortgaged irrevocably to past ideas and present imperatives.

Changing Course, Choosing Peace

The first step in implementing a new policy toward Central America is to cease all support for the contras. The contra war is not only illegal and murderous, it is also the key factor standing in the way of a Contadora treaty. Washington should back such a treaty and pledge to withdraw U.S. military personnel, stop military aid and maneuvers, and in other ways comply with the Contadora provisions. Only with regional demilitarization will economic growth and equitable development become possible.

A major multilateral program of assistance to Central America will be essential, both to repair war damage and to begin and sustain the development process. In Chapter 6, we estimated that after start-up costs of approximately $2 billion, another $16 billion would be needed for development assistance between 1987 and 1992. The United States may reasonably be expected to contribute half, or approximately $9 billion over six years, with the rest coming from other countries and from multilateral institutions such as the World Bank. Admittedly $9 billion is a very substantial sum, but it is considerably less per year than current official U.S. economic and military expenditures in the region.[1]

Postwar assistance, in order to be effective, must be tied to programs that enhance equitable distribution. Massive investments in land reform, health, and education are needed. The United States must use its influence in the World Bank, International Monetary Fund, and Inter-American Development Bank to help design and finance programs of growth-with-equity.

Finally, all U.S. aid should be conditioned on compliance with clear standards of human, political, and labor rights. Popular participation, through political parties, unions, peasant associations,

129

or other mass organizations, must be supported as a positive force for development, not feared as a threat to U.S. interests or security.

The following 12 recommendations summarize the key elements of a new U.S. policy toward Central America. They begin with the most immediate and imperative steps to bring peace to the region, and then build toward longer-range measures to bring about demilitarization, development, and reconciliation. They assume what by now should be apparent: that war is not a shield for development and democracy in Central America; it is an obstacle. As we have emphasized throughout, war and development are incompatible.

I. End the regional war

1. Stop all military, economic, and political efforts to de-stabilize or overthrow the Nicaraguan government; begin by cutting off all assistance to contra forces and abiding by international law.
2. Halt maneuvers in Honduras, cease efforts to militarize Costa Rica, and assist both governments to disarm contra forces within their territories.
3. Cut off all aid for waging war in El Salvador and Guatemala and support negotiated national solutions to the conflicts in those countries.

II. Forge a durable peace

4. Re-open bilateral talks between the United States and Nicaragua and sign a new friendship treaty committing both countries to a mutual nonaggression pact and normalization of relations.
5. Support, and sign a protocol to, a treaty and nonaggression pact among all countries of the region—a treaty that bans foreign bases and military personnel, halts arms imports into Central America and arms smuggling within the region, and provides for reciprocal reductions in military forces.

6. Support efforts for democracy in the region, including free elections in every country, with guarantees of safety for all participants. Support other forms of popular participation in community, labor, and religious organizations.

III. Help rebuild Central America

7. Take the lead in assembling an international program of assistance to rebuild a postwar Central America and provide a basis for renewed, equitable, and environmentally sound growth.
8. Target development assistance to programs that increase the participation of the poor in the region's economies. Support genuine land reform programs, including credits and technical assistance for peasant cooperatives.
9. Condition U.S. aid on compliance with internationally-recognized standards of human, political, and labor rights, as well as respect for indigenous people's culture and tradition. Direct humanitarian assistance to programs run by reputable international organizations or domestic civilian groups, avoiding military-dominated state agencies and programs tied to counterinsurgency activities.
10. Support a rejuvenated Central American Common Market aimed at balanced regional development and the satisfaction of basic needs. Balanced regional development must, in turn, be embedded in more equitable trade and financial relations between Latin America and the United States.

IV. Work for international reconciliation

11. Grant Extended Voluntary Departure status to Central American refugees in the United States instead of detaining and forcibly repatriating them.
12. Foster citizen-to-citizen contact between the United States and Central America through cultural and educational exchanges, "sister city" arrangements, and similar programs designed to exchange skills and promote understanding.

If the Central American conflict can be resolved peacefully, and if the United States can come to accept the realities and positive aspects of nationalism and popular mobilization, a new model of U.S. relations with the Third World may begin to emerge. Central America is indeed a test case—but of a different sort than has been claimed by the Reagan administration.

Demilitarization under Contadora-type guarantees gives hope that other regional conflicts might be settled without further bloodshed. By meeting the demand among major powers for security on their borders, Contadora strengthens the norms of shared responsibility, local initiative, international pluralism, and respect for sovereignty that must prevail if a stable peace is to be established. Demilitarization and peace, in turn, remove many of the threats and insecurities that lead Third World governments to strike Faustian bargains with the superpowers.

Additionally, the changes advocated here will, over the long run, strengthen democracy, both at home and abroad. At home, secrecy and deceit will not be necessary for their implementation, for they do not violate American ideals, public preferences, or constitutional practices. Abroad, policies that take into account the interests and aspirations of the majority will contribute to the popular support that ultimately guarantees all democratic politics.

We are nearing the end of this century. New actors are entering the world stage. People who have been objects of scorn and victims of poverty increasingly demand a voice in deciding their own futures. The United States must find ways to listen to and support these voices, or inevitably it will once again find itself on the side of the dictators, the oligarchs, and the men in uniform.

If we are to contribute to a world governed by law, not by force, a world in which good food, jobs, health, and education are the norm, not the exception, then surely it is best to begin with our own neighbors. Now is the time to demonstrate that the United States can wage peace in Central America just as energetically and determinedly as it has waged war.

132

Note

[1] For a discussion of total costs, see Joshua Cohen and Joel Rogers, *Inequity and Intervention* (Boston: South End Press, 1986), 42–48. Cohen and Rogers estimate that U.S. military activity, including exercises, maneuvers, and the stationing of forces in the region, adds roughly $3 billion a year. If one includes the forces being prepared for use in the region, the overall cost to the tax-payers of military policy in the region reaches $9.5 billion annually.

Economic Growth and External Financing Requirements for Central America: War and Peace Scenarios

Introduction

We have simulated for 1986–92 two contrasting scenarios of Central America's potential for economic growth and for the associated external financing requirements. These scenarios are (1) continued "low-intensity conflict" through 1992 and (2) a negotiated demilitarization in Central America beginning in 1989, consolidated by 1990, with peacetime conditions established in 1991–92.

We have used a "two-gap model" to make these economic simulations. Similar but more sophisticated models of this sort are frequently used by the World Bank and other financial institutions to estimate growth possibilities and the external financial flows from foreign aid, credit, and investment that will be needed to balance national accounts.

In our simulations, we have used economic data from the period 1970–85 for Guatemala, Honduras, El Salvador, Nicaragua, and Costa Rica to generate rough but indicative estimates of the potential for growth both in *a conflicted* and in *a demilitarized Central America*. Our estimates show that a shift in U.S. policy toward a negotiated, demilitarized Central America could lead to impressive economic growth with an external financing bill of close to the combined U.S. economic and military assistance bill estimated for the continuing conflict scenario. As the following chart demonstrates, the opportunity costs of choosing *a conflicted* rather than *a demilitarized Central America* are quite high for Central America.

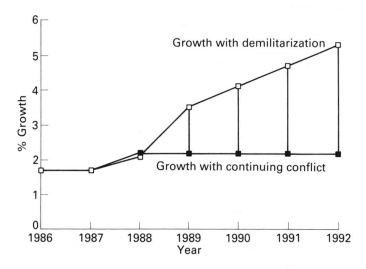

Figure 1 Opportunity Costs of Economic Growth—War vs. Peace

Explanation of the Two-Gap Model

The two-gap model uses two basic identities from standard national macroeconomic accounting frameworks to highlight the effects of the *domestic savings constraint* and the *foreign exchange constraint* on the growth of developing countries. Both can inhibit investment and growth.

• Domestic savings by limiting the availability of funds for investment in future productive facilities.

Appendix A

- Foreign exchange by making unobtainable the capital, intermediate, and consumer goods imports necessary for production and investment.

In the two-gap model, increased availability of foreign aid, credit, and/or investment help to lift the savings constraint as well as the foreign exchange constraint. Increased exports also help lift the foreign exchange constraint, as does relief from debt repayments. In turn, a transfer of expenditures from government consumption or military expenditures to private savings leads to increased investment and economic growth by relaxing the domestic savings constraint.

The model is generally used to estimate the external financing requirements for different target levels of growth. This is done by setting overall economic growth targets, forecasting exports, imports, savings, investment, government spending, and other key variables, and then estimating what the resulting domestic savings and foreign exchange shortfalls will be, given all of the above assumptions and estimates. The foreign assistance that balances the two gaps, the savings gap and the foreign exchange gap, is the external financing requirement necessary for the economic growth targets.

Our simulations used the two-gap model to estimate potential growth rates and the associated external financing requirements. This required us to make assumptions about how additional investment would affect economic growth, since in the two-gap model economic growth estimates are primarily determined by the relationship between investment and additional output. If an additional unit of investment leads to a large expansion in output, then foreign assistance can potentially provide a large stimulus to growth. If an additional unit of investment leads to only a small expansion in output, then foreign assistance might only provide a small stimulus to growth.

Main Results of the Model

Tables 1 and 2 report the growth estimates for each Central American country and the simple average for the region for 1986–92. Table 1 depicts our estimates of growth if current levels of military conflict continue, and Table 2 gives our estimates of growth if a negotiated solution to the main conflicts in the region can be reached. The results are stark.

• Economic growth for the region as a whole in 1986–92 will average 3 to 4 percent per year under peace conditions and less than 2 percent per year under continuing conflict conditions. This was the result represented in Figure 1.
• Per capita economic growth under the scenario of demilitarization will recover and grow by a total of 4 percent over the entire time period. If conflict continues, however, per capita growth will decline by 4 percent over the time period, on top of the more than 33 percent decline already experienced between 1978 and 1985.

Surprisingly enough, the external financing costs of these two scenarios are approximately equal. Under the demilitarization scenario exports increase sufficiently to offset most of the expected growth in demand for imports. Also, the national savings achieved by a shift of expenditures out of military activity help to stimulate the economy without as much external support.

Table 3 presents the external financing costs of the two scenarios. The figures do not include initial reconstruction bills, which are discussed in the text, and which may amount to an additional several billion dollars. The demilitarization scenario has two figures: the larger one includes foreign assistance to Nicaragua, presuming that a peaceful settlement would mean that normal trade and aid relations could be restored.

Despite the large magnitude of external assistance needed to

137

finance the higher levels of growth expected in the demilitarization scenario, the $18 billion figure for U.S., multilateral, and
private support is close to our projection of the cost to the
United States government alone of just maintaining its current
policy. By conservative estimates, current policy will cost the
U.S. government (and the taxpayers) about $15 billion between
1986 and 1992, or more than $2 billion per year over the seven
years.

The annual $2 billion-plus estimate is made by adding to the
1986 figure of approximately $1.1 billion in official U.S. military
and economic aid an additional $1.1 billion annual estimate for
expenses incurred in:

- Conducting land, air, and naval exercises throughout the
  region.
- Basing several thousand U.S. soldiers permanently in Honduras.
- Constructing, maintaining, and equipping airfields, bases,
  and military facilities in the region.
- Training Salvadoran, Honduran, and contra soldiers, as well
  as the Costa Rican national guard.

If this combined estimate of $15 billion in total military and
economic aid expenditures estimate seems too large, note that it
assumes *no growth in official military and economic aid* over the
next seven years, despite the fact that aid figures in 1985 and
1986 are more than five times what they were in 1980. It also
omits any covert spending, which in light of recent revelations
could also inflate "official aid figures."

It is interesting to note here that the Kissinger Commission
Report's analysis led to the estimate that *$24 billion in U.S. and
multilateral assistance* would be needed between 1984 and 1990
if Central America were to achieve 6 percent growth rates by
1990 and a return to living standards near those of 1979. These
estimates, according to the economic analysis given in the
report's Appendix, were based fundamentally on the assump-

tion that violent conflict in the region could be resolved within a short period (one or two years, presumably).

The main body of the Kissinger Report, however, argued for extensive economic growth assistance *in combination with* a major military buildup and expanded counterinsurgency efforts. In effect, the report and subsequent U.S. policy ignored the explicit assumption made by the report's economic analysis— that growth and escalating violent conflict were not compatible—and substituted without mention the implicit assumption that both war and economic recovery and growth were somehow possible.

More than halfway to the 1990 target date of the Kissinger Report, neither its economic growth targets nor its vision of economic recovery is being realized. Instead, violent conflict and high levels of military activity persist throughout Central America, while economic growth per capita continues to decline. Our analysis shows that there is a way out and that it will cost in the neighborhood of what the Kissinger Report estimated in 1984. But this solution depends fundamentally on U.S. willingness to support a demilitarized, negotiated settlement to the crisis in Central America.

Readers wishing more information on formal aspects of the model should contact PACCA at the following address:

Policy Alternatives for the Caribbean and Central America
1506 19th Street N.W. Suite 2
Washington, D.C. 20036

Table 1 Low-Intensity Conflict—Growth of GDP, Aggregate and Per Capita, in Percentages; Debt Figures for 1980, 1985, and 1992 are in U.S. Current Dollars

Country	1980	1985	1986	1987	1988	1989	1990	1991	1992
Costa Rica									
GDP growth	0.8	1.6	2.8	2.9	2.9	2.9	3.0	3.0	3.0
Per capita GDP growth	-2.1	-0.9	-0.2	-0.1	-0.1	-0.1	0.0	0.0	0.0
Foreign debt	$3.2 billion	$4.2 billion							$5.1 billion
Nicaragua									
GDP growth	4.6	-2.6	-1.0	-1.0	1.2	1.4	1.4	1.4	1.4
Per capita GDP growth	1.6	-5.9	-4.0	-4.0	-1.8	-1.6	-1.6	-1.6	-1.6
Foreign debt	$1.8 billion	$4.9 billion							$7.0 billion
Honduras									
GDP growth	2.7	2.6	3.2	3.1	3.0	3.0	3.0	2.9	2.9
Per capita GDP growth	-0.6	-0.6	0.2	0.1	0.0	0.0	0.0	-0.1	-0.1
Foreign debt	$1.4 billion	$2.6 billion							$4.2 billion
El Salvador									
GDP growth	-8.7	1.6	2.3	2.3	2.3	2.3	2.2	2.2	2.2
Per capita GDP growth	-10.3	0.5	1.3	1.3	1.3	1.3	1.2	1.2	1.2
Foreign debt	$1.2 billion	$2.0 billion							$3.0 billion
Guatemala									
GDP growth	3.7	-1.1	1.5	1.5	1.5	1.5	1.6	1.6	1.6
Per capita GDP growth	1	-4	-1.5	-1.5	-1.5	-1.5	-1.4	-1.4	-1.4
Foreign debt	$1.0 billion	$2.6 billion							$4.5 billion
Aver. GDP growth, Central America	0.6	0.4	1.8	1.8	2.2	2.2	2.2	2.2	2.2

Table 2 Negotiations, Peace, and Recovery—Aggregate and Per Capita Growth in Percentages; Debt Figures for 1980, 1985, and 1992 are in Billions of Dollars

Country	1980	1985	1986	1987	1988	1989	1990	1991	1992
Costa Rica									
GDP growth	0.8	1.6	2.8	2.9	2.9	4.0	4.9	5.6	6.6
Per capita GDP growth	-2.1	-0.9	-0.2	-0.1	-0.1	1.0	1.9	2.6	3.6
Foreign debt	$3.2 billion	$4.2 billion							$4.8 billion
Nicaragua									
GDP growth	4.6	-2.6	-1.0	-1.0	1.2	3.9	5.0	5.4	5.9
Per capita GDP growth	1.6	-5.9	-4.0	-4.0	-1.8	0.9	2.0	2.4	2.9
Foreign debt	$1.8 billion	$4.9 billion							$7.0 billion
Honduras									
GDP growth	2.7	2.6	3.2	3.1	2.8	4.6	5.4	6.4	6.3
Per capita GDP growth	-0.6	-0.6	0.2	0.1	-0.2	1.6	2.4	3.4	3.3
Foreign debt	$1.4 billion	$2.6 billion							$4.2 billion
El Salvador									
GDP growth	-8.7	1.6	2.3	2.3	2.0	3.3	3.2	3.7	4.5
Per capita GDP growth	-10.3	0.5	1.3	1.3	1.0	0.3	0.2	0.7	1.5
Foreign debt	$1.2 billion	$2.0 billion							$2.7 billion
Guatemala									
GDP growth	3.7	-1.1	1.5	1.5	1.5	1.9	2.2	2.5	2.9
Per capita GDP growth	1	-4	-1.5	-1.5	-1.5	-1.1	-0.8	-0.5	-0.1
Foreign debt	$1.0 billion	$2.6 billion							$4.4 billion
Aver. GDP growth, Central America	0.62	0.4	1.8	1.8	2.1	3.5	4.1	4.7	5.2

Table 3 External Financing Costs of Growth Scenarios and the Cost of Continuing Current U.S. Policy, 1986–92

Scenario	*External Financing Required to Meet Balance of Payments (in $ billions)*	*Expenses of U.S. Aid and Military Involvement under Current Policy (in $ billions)*
Continuing low-intensity conflict scenario	16.4	15.4[a]
Demilitarized Central America:		
with aid to Nicaragua	18.3[b]	
with no aid to Nicaragua	15.6	

[a] Estimate of U.S. expenses is made by taking official aid figures of $1.1 billion per year and adding $1.1 billion annually for expenses of military involvement. There is overlap of official economic aid figures of about $1 billion per year between the figures for external financing requirements of continuing conflict and estimated U.S. expenses for aid and military involvement. Still, the overall cost of current policy is significantly higher than a demilitarization policy would be.

[b] This figure includes Nicaragua's external financing needs for the 1986–92 period.

APPENDIX B

Central America in Figures

Central America: Selected Social Statistics

	Costa Rica	El Salvador	Guatemala	Honduras	Nicaragua
Population in 1985[a] (millions)	2.52	4.86	7.96	4.40	3.27
GNP per capita (US$)[b]	1,020	710	1,120	670	880
Infant mortality per thousand live births[b]	20	70	67	81	84
Life expectancy[a]	73	57	59	62	60
Population per physician[b]	2,740	5,330	4,640	12,620	2,690
Literacy (percentage)[a]	90	67	56	60	88

[a] Inter-American Development Bank, *Economic and Social Progress in Latin America 1986.*
[b] World Bank, *Social Indicators Data Sheet, June 1985.*

Central America: Income Distribution
(Percentage of national income by stratum, late 1970s)

	Costa Rica	El Salvador	Guatemala	Honduras	Nicaragua
Poorest 20%	4	2	5	4	3
30% below mean	17	10	15	13	13
30% above mean	30	22	26	24	26
Wealthiest 20%	49	66	54	60	58

Source: United Nations Economic Commission for Latin America, *The Crisis in Central America: Its Origins, Scope, and Consequences*, 15 September 1983, 14.

Appendix B

Distribution of Land in Central America

	Percentage of Land Belonging to Farms With Less Than 10 Hectares[a]		Percentage of Land Belonging to Farms With More Than 100 Hectares[a]	
	1960–70	*1970–80*	*1960–70*	*1970–80*
Costa Rica	4.7	3.8	62.3	67.2
El Salvador	21.8	27.1	47.7	38.7
Guatemala[b]	20.0	16.0	62.0	65.0
Honduras[c]	16.0	17.0	57.0	55.0
Nicaragua[d]	2.0	10.5[e]	52.5	26.5[f]

[a] For each observation the decade is given rather than the exact year. One hectare equals 2.47 acres.

[b] Farm size limits for the two categories are less than 10 manzanas (1 manzana = 0.7 hectares) and more than 64 manzanas.

[c] 1960–70 figures refer to 1954.

[d] 1970–80 figures refer to 1983; farm size limits for the two categories are less than 10 manzanas and more than 200 manzanas.

[e] Also includes production cooperatives of small-scale farmers.

[f] Excludes state-owned farms.

Source: Peter Peek, *Rural Poverty in Central America: Causes and Policy Alternatives* (Geneva: International Labour Office, 1986).

Distribution of Land in El Salvador

Farm Size (hectares)	Number of Farms	Percentage of Farms	Number of Hectares	Percentage of All Farmland
0–2	191,527	70.9	151,324	10.4
2–10	59,012	21.8	242,455	16.7
10–100	18,388	6.8	496,593	34.1
100+	1,941	0.7	561,518	38.7

Source: 1971 Agricultural Census, El Salvador.

144

Central America: Growth of Gross Domestic Product

	1981	1982	1983	1984	1985	1986	Cumulative variation, 1981–86
Costa Rica	-2.4	-7.3	2.7	7.9	0.9	3.0	4.0
El Salvador	-8.4	-5.7	0.6	1.4	1.4	-0.5	-11.1
Guatemala	1.0	-3.4	-2.7	0.0	-0.9	0.0	-6.0
Honduras	1.0	-1.6	-0.6	3.1	1.4	2.0	5.5
Nicaragua	5.4	-0.8	4.4	-1.4	-2.6	0.0	5.0
Latin America	0.5	-1.4	-2.4	3.2	2.7	3.4	5.9

Source: United Nations Economic Commission for Latin America and the Caribbean, *Preliminary Overview of the Latin American Economy 1986*, 13.

145

Central America: Growth of Per Capita Gross Domestic Product

	1981	1982	1983	1984	1985	1986	*Cumulative variation, 1981–86*
Costa Rica	-5.0	-9.7	0.0	5.1	-1.7	0.4	-11.0
El Salvador	-9.6	-6.5	0.2	0.5	0.1	-1.8	-16.7
Guatemala	-1.8	-6.1	-5.4	2.8	-3.7	-2.8	-20.7
Honduras	-2.4	-4.9	-3.9	-0.3	-1.8	-1.2	-13.8
Nicaragua	2.0	-4.4	1.3	-4.8	-5.9	-3.1	-14.1
Latin America	0.5	-1.4	-2.4	3.2	2.7	3.4	5.9

Source: United Nations Economic Commission for Latin America and the Caribbean, *Preliminary Overview of the Latin American Economy 1986*, 14.

U.S. Aid to Central America (in $ millions)

Guatemala

FY[a]	DA[a]	PL480[a]	Other[a]	Economic Total	ESF[a]	IMET[a]	FMS[a]	MAP[a]	Security Total	Total
80	7.8	3.3	—	11.1	—	—	—	—	—	11.1
81	9.1	7.5	—	16.6	—	—	—	—	—	16.6
82	8.2	5.6	1.7	15.5	—	—	—	—	—	15.5
83	12.3	5.4	2.0	19.7	10.0	—	—	—	10.0	29.7
84	4.5	13.2	2.6	20.3	—	—	—	—	—	20.3
85	63.2	28.2	3.0	94.4	12.5	0.5	—	—	13.0	107.4
86	36.9	15.0	5.8	57.7	47.8	0.4	—	5.0	53.2	110.9
87[b]	33.3	19.0	5.3	57.6	58.8	0.4	—	2.0	61.2	118.8
88[c]	33.3	18.0	7.7	59.0	80.0	0.6	—	5.0	85.6	144.6

Honduras

FY	DA	PL480	Other	Economic Total	ESF	IMET	FMS	MAP	Security Total	Total
80	45.8	5.2	—	51.0	—	0.4	3.5	—	4.0	55.0
81	25.7	8.2	—	33.9	—	0.5	8.4	—	8.9	42.8
82	31.1	10.1	2.7	43.9	36.8	1.3	19.0	11.0	68.1	112.0
83	31.3	15.5	3.2	50.0	56.0	0.8	9.0	38.5	104.3	154.3
84	31.0	20.2	3.8	55.0	40.0	0.9	—	76.5	117.4	172.4
85	54.4	19.4	5.0	78.8	150.2	1.1	—	66.3	217.6	296.4
86	44.3	13.8	4.6	62.7	61.3	1.0	—	60.1	122.4	185.1
87[b]	40.3	12.0	5.0	57.3	71.4	1.2	—	60.0	132.6	189.9
88[c]	40.3	12.0	4.4	56.7	100.0	1.5	—	80.0	181.5	238.2

U.S. Aid to Central America (in $ millions) (*continued*)

El Salvador

FY	DA	PL480	Other	Economic Total	ESF	IMET	FMS	MAP	Security Total	Total
80	43.2	5.5	—	48.7	9.1	0.2	5.7	—	15.0	63.7
81	33.3	35.4	—	68.7	44.9	0.5	10.0	25.0	80.4	149.1
82	39.6	27.6	—	67.2	115.0	2.0	16.5	63.5	197.0	264.2
83	58.8	46.8	—	105.6	140.0	1.3	46.3	33.5	221.1	326.7
84	41.2	54.5	—	95.7	120.2	1.3	18.5	176.8	316.8	412.5
85	91.1	57.8	—	148.9	285.0	1.5	10.0	124.8	421.3	570.2
86	84.0	44.0	10.4	138.4	177.0	1.4	—	120.3	298.7	437.1
87[b]	75.6	42.0	209.5	327.1	181.8	1.5	—	115.0	298.3	625.4
88[c]	75.6	35.0	8.7	119.3	200.0	1.9	—	120.0	321.9	441.2

Nicaragua

FY	DA	PL480	Other	Economic Total	ESF	IMET	FMS	MAP	Security Total	Total
80	18.3	17.6	0.1	36.0	1.1	—	—	—	1.1	37.1
81	1.8	1.2	0.1	3.1	56.6	—	—	—	56.6	59.7
82	0.7	0.4	0.1	1.2	5.1	—	—	—	5.1	6.3
83	—	—	—	—	—	—	—	—	—	—
84	—	—	0.1	0.1	—	—	—	—	—	0.1
85	—	—	—	—	—	—	—	—	—	—
86	—	—	—	—	—	—	—	—	—	—
87[b]	—	—	—	—	—	—	—	—	—	—
88[c]	—	—	—	—	—	—	—	—	—	—

Costa Rica

FY	DA	PL480	Other	Economic Total	ESF	IMET	FMS	MAP	Security Total	Total
80	13.6	0.4	—	14.0	—	—	—	—	—	14.0
81	11.5	1.8	—	13.3	—	—	—	—	—	13.3
82	11.5	19.1	1.1	31.7	20.0	0.1	—	2.0	22.1	53.8
83	27.2	28.2	1.7	57.1	157.0	0.1	—	4.5	161.6	218.7
84	15.5	22.5	1.9	39.9	130.0	0.1	—	9.0	139.1	179.0
85	25.9	21.6	2.9	50.4	169.6	0.2	—	11.0	180.8	231.2
86	11.0	16.2	0.3	27.5	120.5	0.2	—	2.4	123.1	150.6
87[b]	12.8	16.0	0.2	29.0	87.8	0.2	—	1.5	89.5	118.5
88[c]	12.8	15.0	0.2	28.0	90.0	0.5	—	2.0	92.5	120.5

Five Countries

FY	DA	PL480	Other	Economic Total	ESF	IMET	FMS	MAP	Security Total	Total
80	128.7	32.0	0.1	160.8	10.2	0.6	9.2	0.0	20.1	180.9
81	81.4	54.1	0.1	135.6	101.5	1.0	18.4	25.0	145.9	281.5
82	91.1	62.8	5.6	159.5	176.9	3.4	35.5	76.5	292.3	451.8
83	129.6	95.9	6.9	232.4	363.0	2.2	55.3	76.5	497.0	729.4
84	92.2	110.4	8.4	211.0	290.2	2.3	18.5	262.3	573.3	784.3
85	234.6	127.0	10.9	372.4	617.3	3.3	10.0	202.1	832.7	1205.2
86	176.2	89.0	21.1	286.3	406.6	3.0	0.0	187.8	597.4	883.7
87[b]	162.0	89.0	220.0	471.0	399.8	3.3	0.0	178.5	581.6	1052.6
88[c]	162.0	80.0	21.0	263.0	470.0	4.5	0.0	207.0	681.5	944.5

[*For notes and sources, see p. 150*]

Appendix B

Notes and Sources

   a Explanation of categories:
FY: Fiscal Year
DA: Development Aid
PL480: Subsidized Food Sales and Grants
Other: includes Peace Corps, narcotics control, and disaster relief
ESF: Economic Support Fund
IMET: International Military Education and Training
FMS: Foreign Military Sales (Credit Financing)
MAP: Military Assistance Program
   b Estimates
   c Administration Requests

Sources: Agency for International Development. *U.S. Overseas Loans, Grants and Assistance from International Organizations* and *Fiscal Year 1988— Summary Tables*, January 1987.

Index

For explanation of acronyms, see under main entry.

Index

Index by
Elizabeth A. Clutton